the

GREAT
HOUSE
of GOD

ALSO BY MAX LUCADO

the
GREAT
HOUSE
of GOD

A Home for Your Heart

Max Lucado

THOMAS NELSON
Since 1798

NASHVILLE   DALLAS   MEXICO CITY   RIO DE JANEIRO

Published in Nashville, Tennessee, by Thomas Nelson. Thomas Nelson is a registered trademark of Thomas Nelson, Inc.

Thomas Nelson, Inc. titles may be purchased in bulk for educational, business, fund-raising, or sales promotional use. For information, please e-mail SpecialMarkets@ThomasNelson.com.

Unless otherwise noted, Scripture quotations are taken from the New Century Version®. © 2005 by Thomas Nelson, Inc. Used by permission. All rights reserved.

Other Scripture references are from the following sources: Holy Bible, New International Version®, NIV® (NIV). © 1973, 1978, 1984 by Biblica, Inc.™ Used by permission of Zondervan. All rights reserved worldwide. King James Version of the Bible (KJV). New American Standard Bible® (NASB), © The Lockman Foundation 1960, 1962, 1963, 1968, 1971, 1972, 1973, 1975, 1977, 1995. Used by permission. The Living Bible (TLB), © 1971 by Tyndale House Publishers, Wheaton, IL. Used by permission. The Message by Eugene H. Peterson (MSG). © 1993, 1994, 1995, 1996, 2000, 2002. Used by permission of NavPress Publishing Group. All rights reserved. New King James Version® (NKJV). © 1982 by Thomas Nelson, Inc. Used by permission. All rights reserved. J. B. Phillips: The New Testament in Modern English, Revised Edition (PHILLIPS). © J. B. Phillips 1958, 1960, 1972. Used by permission of Macmillan Publishing Co., Inc. Revised Standard Version of the Bible (RSV). © 1946, 1952, 1971, 1973 by the Division of Christian Education of the National Council of the Churches of Christ in the USA. Used by permission. The Jerusalem Bible (TJB). © 1968 by Darton, Longman, & Todd, Ltd., and Doubleday & Co., Inc. Used by permission. New English Bible (NEB). © 1961, 1970 by the delegates of the Oxford University Press and the Syndics of the Cambridge University Press. Reprinted by permission.

ISBN 978-0-8499-4746-9 (repackage)
ISBN 0-8499-4081-8 (trade paper)
ISBN 0-8499-3995-X (Special Edition)

Library of Congress has cataloged the earlier edition as follows:

Lucado, Max
    The great house of God: a home for your heart / Max Lucado.
        p. cm.
    Includes bibliographical references
    ISBN 0-8499-1295-4 (hardcover)
    1. Lord's prayer. I. Title
BV230.173 1997
226.9'606—dc21   97-22821
CIP

Printed in the United States of America

13 14 15 16 17 QG 5 4 3 2

*I gladly dedicate this book to my assistant, Karen Hill.
Thank you for thousands of hours of selfless service.*

Contents

Acknowledgments ix

1 The Great House of God: A Home for Your Heart 1
2 The Living Room: When Your Heart Needs a Father 9
3 The Foundation: Where Trust Begins 21
4 The Observatory: A Heavenly Affection 31
5 The Chapel: Where Man Covers His Mouth 43
6 The Throne: Touching the King's Heart 51
7 The Study: How God Reveals His Will 61
8 The Furnace: Because Someone Prayed 73
9 The Kitchen: God's Abundant Table 83
10 The Roof: Beneath God's Grace 95
11 The Hallway: Grace Received, Grace Given 105
12 The Family Room: Learning to Live Together 117
13 The Walls: Satan, God's Servant 127
14 The Chapel: Relying on God's Power 141
15 A Home for Your Heart 151

The Bedroom—God doesn't sleep

Postscript: His Model, Our Guide 157

NO Bedroom

Notes 161

Study Guide 163

ACKNOWLEDGMENTS

I appreciate the following friends for helping, tolerating, resuscitating, and/or indulging me during the writing of this book:

Liz Heaney—Yet another book, yet another year and still no regrets.

The Oak Hills Church leadership and staff—I'm out of hibernation! Thanks for covering for me.

The Oak Hills Church—Thanks for ten years (!) of joy.

Steve and Cheryl Green—I don't know what I did to deserve friends like you, but I'm sure glad I did it.

All my friends at Thomas Nelson—A hearty thanks for a job well done.

To all my minister friends who use my stuff for sermon ideas—Power to you! You deserve a break.

To Laura Kendall—A tip o' the hat for your dip o' the quill. Thanks for your help.

Steve Halliday—For writing the discussion guide.

And *to the readers*—Some of you I'm meeting for the first time, others for the twelfth. You are so gracious to invite me into your home. I'll do my best not to overstay my welcome.

And lastly, to my wife, Denalyn—I guess you could say I love you a little. A little more every minute of every day. (Happy 40th, honey!)

CHAPTER 1

THE GREAT HOUSE OF GOD

A HOME FOR YOUR HEART

I ask only one thing from the Lord.
This is what I want: Let me live in the Lord's house all my life.

—PSALM 27:4

I'd like to talk with you about your house. Let's step through the front door and walk around a bit. Every so often it's wise to do a home inspection; you know—check the roof for leaks and examine the walls for bows and the foundation for cracks. We'll see if your kitchen cupboards are full and glance at the books on the shelves in your study.

What's that? You think it odd that I want to look at your house? You thought this was a book on spiritual matters? It is. Forgive me, I should have been clearer. I'm not talking about your visible house of stone or sticks, wood or straw, but your invisible one of thoughts and truths and convictions and hopes. I'm talking about your spiritual house.

You have one, you know. And it's no typical house. Conjure up your fondest notions and this house exceeds them all. A grand castle has been built for your heart. Just as a physical house exists to care for the body, so the spiritual house exists to care for your soul.

You've never seen a house more solid:
the roof never leaks,
   the walls never crack,
      and the foundation never trembles.
You've never seen a castle more splendid:
the observatory will stretch you,
   the chapel will humble you,
      the study will direct you,
         and the kitchen will nourish you.

Ever lived in a house like this? Chances are you haven't. Chances are you've given little thought to housing your soul. We create elaborate houses for our bodies, but our souls are relegated to a hillside shanty where the night winds chill us and the rain soaks us. Is it any wonder the world is so full of cold hearts?

Doesn't have to be this way. We don't have to live outside. It's not God's plan for your heart to roam as a Bedouin. God wants you to move in out of the cold and live . . . with him. Under his roof there is space available. At his table a plate is set. In his living room a wingback chair is reserved just for you. And he'd like you to take up residence in his house. Why would he want you to share his home?

Simple. He's your Father.

You were intended to live in your Father's house. Any place less than his is insufficient. Any place far from his is dangerous. Only the home built for your heart can protect your heart. And your Father wants you to dwell *in* him.

No, you didn't misread the sentence, and I didn't miswrite it. Your Father doesn't just ask you to live *with* him, he asks you to live *in* him.

As Paul wrote, "For in him we live and move and have our being" (Acts 17:28 NIV).

Don't think you are separated from God, he at the top end of a great ladder, you at the other. Dismiss any thought that God is on Venus while you are on Earth. Since God is Spirit (John 4:24), he is next to you: God himself is our roof. God himself is our wall. And God himself is our foundation.

Moses knew this. "Lord," he prayed, "you have been our home since the beginning" (Ps. 90:1). What a powerful thought: God as your home. Your home is the place where you can kick off your shoes and eat pickles and crackers and not worry about what people think when they see you in your bathrobe.

Your home is familiar to you. No one has to tell you how to locate your bedroom; you don't need directions to the kitchen. After a hard day scrambling to find your way around in the world, it's assuring to come home to a place you know. God can be equally familiar to you. With time you can learn where to go for nourishment, where to hide for protection, where to turn for guidance. Just as your earthly house is a place of refuge, so God's house is a place of peace. God's house has never been plundered; his walls have never been breached.

God can be your dwelling place.

God *wants* to be your dwelling place. He has no interest in being a weekend getaway or a Sunday bungalow or a summer cottage. Don't consider using God as a vacation cabin or an eventual retirement home. He wants you under his roof now and always. He wants to be your mailing address, your point of reference; he wants to be your home. Listen to the promise of his Son: "If my people love me they will obey my teaching. My Father will love them and we will come to them and make our home with them" (John 14:23).

For many this is a new thought. We think of God as a deity to discuss, not a place to dwell. We think of God as a mysterious miracle worker, not a house to live in. We think of God as the Creator to call on, not a home to reside in. But our Father wants to be much more. He wants to be the One in whom "we live and move and have our being" (Acts 17:28 NIV).

When Jehovah led the children of Israel through the wilderness, he didn't just appear once a day and then abandon them. The pillar of fire was present all night; the cloud was present all day. Our God never leaves us. "I will be with you always," he promised (Matt. 28:20). Our faith takes a quantum leap when we understand the perpetual presence of the Father. Our Jehovah is the fire of our night and the cloud of our day. He never leaves us.

Heaven knows no difference between Sunday morning and Wednesday afternoon. God longs to speak as clearly in the workplace as he does in the sanctuary. He longs to be worshiped when we sit at the dinner table and not just when we come to his communion table. You may go days without thinking of him, but there's never a moment when he's not thinking of you.

Knowing this, we understand Paul's rigorous goal: "We capture every thought and make it give up and obey Christ" (2 Cor. 10:5). We can fathom why he urged us to "pray without ceasing" (1 Thess. 5:17 NKJV), "be constant in prayer" (Rom. 12:12 RSV), "pray in the Spirit at all times" (Eph. 6:18), "continually offer the sacrifice of praise to God" (Heb. 13:15 NKJV), and "let heaven fill your thoughts" (Col. 3:2 TLB).

David, the man after God's own heart, said, "I'm asking GOD for one thing, only one thing: to live with him in his house my whole life long. I'll contemplate his beauty; I'll study at his feet. That's the only quiet, secure place in a noisy world" (Ps. 27:4–5 MSG). What is this house of God that David seeks? Is David describing a physical struc-ture? Does he long for a building with four walls and a door through which he can enter but never exit? No. Our Lord "does not live in temples built by human hands" (Acts 17:24). When David said, "I will live in the house of the LORD forever" (Ps. 23:6), he was not saying he wanted to get away from people. He was saying that he yearned to be in God's presence, wherever he was.

David longed to be in God's house.

I know what you're thinking: *Sure, Max, but he was David. He was the poet, the prince, the giant-killer. He didn't have car pools and diapers and a boss who breathes deadlines like a dragon breathes fire. I'd love to live in God's house, too, but for the time being, I'm stuck in the* real *world.*

Forgive me, but I beg to differ. You aren't stuck in the real world. Just the opposite, you are one step away from the house of God. Wherever you are. Whatever time it is. Whether in the office on Thursday or at soccer practice on Saturday, you are only a decision away from the presence of your Father. You need never leave the house of God. You don't need to change your zip code or your neighborhood; all you need to change is your perception.

When your car is stuck in traffic, you can step into the chapel. When the gust of temptation unbalances your stride, step behind the wall of his strength. When the employees belittle you, take a seat in the porch swing next to your Father; he'll comfort you. Remember, this is no house of stone. You won't find it on a map. You won't find it described in a realtor journal.

But you will find it in your Bible. You've seen the blueprint before. You've read the names of the rooms and recited the layout. You're familiar with the design. But chances are you never considered it to be a house plan. You viewed the verses as a prayer.

Indeed they are. The Lord's Prayer. It would be difficult to find someone who hasn't quoted the prayer or read the words:

Our Father which art in heaven, Hallowed be thy name.
Thy kingdom come, Thy will be done in earth, as it is in heaven.
Give us this day our daily bread.
And forgive us our debts, as we forgive our debtors.

And lead us not into temptation, but deliver us from evil: For thine is
the kingdom, and the power, and the glory, for ever. Amen.
(MATTHEW 6:9–13 KJV)

Children memorize it. Parishioners recite it. Students study it . . .
but I want to challenge us to do something different. I want us to live
in it . . . to view it as the floor plan to our spiritual house. In these
verses Christ has provided more than a model for prayer, he has provided a model for living. These words do more than tell us what to
say to God; they tell us how to exist with God. These words describe
a grand house in which God's children were intended to live . . . with
him, forever.

Would you like to take a look around? Me too. I know the perfect
place to begin. In the living room a painting hangs over the mantel.
The owner of the house treasures it. He invites all who enter to begin
their journey gazing at the picture and learning the truth about our
Father.

CHAPTER 2

The Living Room

WHEN YOUR HEART NEEDS A FATHER

Our Father . . .

O ur Father who is in heaven . . ." (Matt. 6:9 NASB). With these words Jesus escorts us into the Great House of God. Shall we follow him? There is so much to see. Every room reveals his heart; every stop will soothe your soul. And no room is as essential as this one we enter first. Walk behind him as he leads us into God's living room.

Sit in the chair that was made for you, and warm your hands by the fire that never fades. Take time to look at the framed photos and find yours. Be sure to pick up the scrapbook and find the story of your life. But please, before any of that, stand at the mantel and study the painting that hangs above it.

Your Father treasures the portrait. He has hung it where all can see.

Stand before it a thousand times and each gaze is as fresh as the first. Let a million look at the canvas and each one will see himself. And each will be right.

Captured in the portrait is a tender scene of a father and a son.

Behind them is a great house on a hill. Beneath their feet is a narrow path. Down from the house the father has run. Up the trail the son has trudged. The two have met, here, at the gate.

We can't see the face of the son; it's buried in the chest of his father. No, we can't see his face, but we can see his tattered robe and stringy hair. We can see the mud on the back of his legs, the filth on his shoulders, and the empty purse on the ground. At one time the purse was full of money. At one time the boy was full of pride. But that was a dozen taverns ago. Now both the purse and the pride are depleted. The prodigal offers no gift or explanation. All he offers is the smell of pigs and a rehearsed apology: "Father, I have sinned against God and against you. I am no longer worthy to be called your son" (Luke 15:21).

He feels unworthy of his birthright. "Demote me. Punish me. Take my name off the mailbox and my initials off the family tree. I am willing to give up my place at your table." The boy is content to be a hired hand. There is only one problem. Though the boy is willing to stop being a son, the father is not willing to stop being a father.

Though we can't see the boy's face in the painting, we can't miss the father's. Look at the tears glistening on the leathered cheeks, the smile shining through the silver beard. One arm holds the boy up so he won't fall, the other holds the boy close so he won't doubt.

"Hurry!" he shouts. "Bring the best clothes and put them on him. Also, put a ring on his finger and sandals on his feet. And get our fat calf and kill it so we can have a feast and celebrate. My son was dead, but now he is alive again! He was lost, but now he is found!" (Luke 15:22–24).

How these words must have stunned the young man, "My son was dead . . ." He thought he'd lost his place in the home. After all, didn't he abandon his father? Didn't he waste his inheritance? The boy assumed he had forfeited his privilege to sonship. The father, however, doesn't give up that easily. In his mind, his son is still a son. The child may have been out of the house, but he was never out of his father's heart. He may have left the table, but he never left the family. Don't miss the message here. You may be willing to stop being God's child. But God is not willing to stop being your Father.

OUR *Abba*

Of all his names, *Father* is God's favorite. We know he loves this name most because this is the one he used most. While on earth Jesus called God "Father" over two hundred times. In his first recorded words Jesus explained, "Didn't you know that I must be in my Father's house?" (Luke 2:49). In his final triumphant prayer he proclaimed, "Father, I give you my life" (Luke 23:46). In the gospel of John alone, Jesus repeats this name 156 times. God loves to be called Father. After all, didn't Jesus teach us to begin our prayer with the phrase, "Our *Abba*"?

It is difficult for us to understand how revolutionary it was for Jesus to call Jehovah "Abba." What is a common practice today was unheard of in Jesus' day. New Testament scholar Joachim Jeremias describes how rarely the term was used:

> With the help of my assistants, I have examined the prayer litera-
> ture of ancient Judaism. . . . The result of this examination was,
> that in no place in this immense literature is this invocation of
> God as "Abba, Father" to be found. Abba was an everyday word.
> It was a homely family-word. No Jew would have dared to address
> God in this manner, yet Jesus did it always in all his prayers which
> are handed down to us, with one single exception: the cry from
> the cross, "My God, my God, why have you forsaken me?" In the

Lord's Prayer, Jesus authorizes his disciples to repeat the word *Abba* after him. He gives them a share in his sonship. He empowers his disciples to speak with their heavenly father in such a familiar and trusting way.[1]

The first two words of the Lord's Prayer are affluent in significance: "Our Father" reminds us we are welcome in God's house because we have been adopted by the owner.

GOD'S MISSION: ADOPTION

When we come to Christ, God not only forgives us, he also adopts us. Through a dramatic series of events, we go from condemned orphans with no hope to adopted children with no fear. Here is how it happens. You come before the judgment seat of God full of rebellion and mistakes. Because of his justice he cannot dismiss your sin, but because of his love he cannot dismiss you. So in an act that stunned the heavens, he punished himself on the cross for your sins. God's justice and love are equally honored. And you, God's creation, are forgiven. But the story doesn't end with God's forgiveness.

> For you have not received a spirit of slavery leading to fear again, but you have received a spirit of adoption as sons by which we cry out, "Abba! Father!" The Spirit Himself testifies with our spirit that we are children of God. (Rom. 8:15–16 NASB)

> But when the fullness of the time came, God sent forth His Son, born of a woman, born under the Law, so that He might redeem those who were under the Law, that we might receive the adoption as sons. (Gal. 4:4–5 NASB)

It would be enough if God just cleansed your name, but he does more. He gives you *his* name. It would be enough if God just set you free, but he does more. He takes you home. He takes you home to the Great House of God.

Adoptive parents understand this more than anyone. I certainly don't mean to offend any biological parents—I'm one myself. We biological parents know well the earnest longing to have a child. But in many cases our cribs were filled easily. We decided to have a child and a child came. In fact, sometimes the child came with no decision. I've heard of unplanned pregnancies, but I've never heard of an unplanned adoption.

That's why adoptive parents understand God's passion to adopt us. They know what it means to feel an empty space inside. They know what it means to hunt, to set out on a mission, and take responsibility for a child with a spotted past and a dubious future. If anybody understands God's ardor for his children, it's someone who has rescued an orphan from despair, for that is what God has done for us.

God has adopted you. God sought you, found you, signed the papers, and took you home.

GOD'S MOTIVE: DEVOTION

As a minister I have had the privilege of witnessing—up close—the emotion of adoption. On one occasion a lady in another state who had heard me speak called and asked if I knew any prospective adoptive parents. Her pregnant daughter was seeking a home for her unborn child. I put her in touch with a family from our congregation and took a front row seat as the drama unfolded.

I saw the joy at the possibility and the heartbreak at the roadblocks. I watched the resolve in the eyes of the father and the determination in the eyes of the mother. They would travel as far as it took and spend every penny they had. They wanted to adopt that child. And they did. Only moments after his birth, the infant was placed in their arms. And this is no exaggeration: They smiled for a month after they brought their son home. I'd see them in the church hallway; they'd be smiling. I'd see them in the parking lot, smiling. From the pulpit I could see them in the congregation, cradling the baby and smiling. I think if I'd preached a sermon on the agony of hell, they would have smiled through every sentence. Why? Because the child they had longed for had come into their home.

Let me ask you, why did this couple adopt that child? They had a happy marriage. They were financially secure and gainfully employed. What did they hope to gain? Did they adopt the baby so they might have a little extra cash or sleep? You know better. Their supply of both diminished the minute they brought the child home. Then why? Why do people adopt children? As you are thinking, let me tell you why God does.

Delight in these words:

> Long ago, before God made the world, God chose us to be his very own, through what Christ would do for us; he decided then to make us holy in his eyes, without a single fault we who stand before him covered in his love. His unchanging plan has always been to adopt us into his own family by sending Jesus Christ to die for us. *And he did this because he wanted to.* (Eph. 1:3–5 TLB, emphasis mine)

And you thought God adopted you because you were good-looking. You thought he needed your money or your wisdom. Sorry. God adopted you simply because he wanted to. You were in his good will and pleasure. Knowing full well the trouble you would be and the price he would pay, he signed his name next to yours and changed your name to his and took you home. Your *Abba* adopted you and became your Father.

May I pause here for just a second? Most of you are with me . . . but a couple of you are shaking your heads. I see those squinty eyes. You don't believe me, do you? You're waiting for the fine print. There's got to be a gimmick. You know life has no free lunch, so you're waiting for the check.

Your discomfort is obvious. Even here in God's living room, you never unwind. Others put on slippers, you put on a front. Others relax, you stiffen. Always on your best behavior, ever anxious that you'll slip up and God will notice and out you'll go.

I understand your anxiety. Our experience with people has taught us that what is promised and what is presented aren't always the same. And for some, the thought of trusting a heavenly Father is doubly difficult because your earthly father disappointed or mistreated you.

If such is the case, I urge you: Don't confuse your heavenly Father with the fathers you've seen on earth. Your Father in heaven isn't prone to headaches and temper tantrums. He doesn't hold you one day and hit you the next. The man who fathered you may play such games, but the God who loves you never will. May I prove my point?

GOD'S METHOD: REDEMPTION

Let's return to the verses that describe your adoption. Read them a second time and see if you can find the verb that precedes the word *adoption* in both verses.

> For you have not received a spirit of slavery leading to fear again, but
> you have received a spirit of adoption as sons by which we cry out,

"Abba! Father!" The Spirit Himself testifies with our spirit that we
are children of God. (Rom. 8:15–16 NASB)

But when the fullness of the time came, God sent forth His Son,
born of a woman, born under the Law, so that He might redeem
those who were under the Law, that we might receive the adoption
as sons. (Gal. 4:4–5 NASB)

Find it? Not too hard to see, is it? Before the word *adoption* is the
word *receive*.

Could Paul have used another phrase? Could he have said, "You
have earned the spirit of adoption"? Or "that we might earn our adoption as sons"? I suppose he could have, but we wouldn't have bought
it. You and I both know that an adoption is not something we earn;
it's something we receive. To be adopted into a family is not a feat one
achieves but rather a gift one accepts.

The parents are the active ones. Adoption agencies don't train
children to recruit parents; they seek parents to adopt children. The
parents make the call and fill out the papers and endure the interviews and pay the fee and wait the wait. Can you imagine prospective
parents saying, "We'd like to adopt Johnny, but first we want to know
a few things. Does he have a house to live in? Does he have money
for tuition? Does he have a ride to school every morning and clothes
to wear every day? Can he prepare his own meals and mend his own
clothes?"

No agency would stand for such talk. Its representative would lift
her hand and say, "Wait a minute. You don't understand. You don't
adopt Johnny because of what he has; you adopt him because of what
he needs. He needs a home."

The same is true with God. He doesn't adopt us because of what we
have. He doesn't give us his name because of our wit or wallet or good

attitude. Paul stated it twice because he was doubly concerned that we understand that adoption is something we receive, not something we earn.

Which is *so good* to know. Why? Think carefully about this. If we can't earn our adoption by our stellar performance, can we lose it through our poor performance?

When I was seven years old, I ran away from home. I'd had enough of my father's rules and decided I could make it on my own, thank you very much. With my clothes in a paper bag, I stormed out the back gate and marched down the alley. Like the prodigal son, I decided I needed no father. Unlike the prodigal son, I didn't go far. I got to the end of the alley and remembered I was hungry, so I went back home.

But though the rebellion was brief, it was rebellion nonetheless. And had you stopped me on that prodigal path between the fences and asked me who my father was, I just might have told you how I felt. I just might have said, "I don't need a father. I'm too big for the rules of my family. It's just me, myself, and my paper bag." I don't remember saying that to anyone, but I remember thinking it. And I also remember rather sheepishly stepping in the back door and taking my seat at the supper table across from the very father I had, only moments before, disowned.

Did he know of my insurrection? I suspect he did. Did he know of my denial? Dads usually do. Was I still his son? Apparently so. (No one else was sitting in my place.) Had you gone to my father after you had spoken to me and asked, "Mr. Lucado, your son says he has no need of a father. Do you still consider him your son?" what would my dad have said?

I don't have to guess at his answer. He called himself my father even when I didn't call myself his son. His commitment to me was greater than my commitment to him.

I didn't hear the rooster crow as Peter did. I didn't feel the fish belch as Jonah did. I didn't get a robe and a ring and sandals as the prodigal did. But I learned from my father on earth what those three learned from their Father in heaven. Our God is no fair-weather Father. He's not into this love-'em-and-leave-'em-stuff. I can count on him to be in my corner no matter how I perform. You can too.

May I show you something? Look at the bottom of the painting. See the words etched in gold? The apostle Paul penned them, but your Father inspired them.

> Neither death, nor life, nor angels, nor ruling spirits, nothing now, nothing in the future, no powers, nothing above us, nothing below us, nor anything else in the whole world will ever be able to sepa-rate us from the love of God that is in Christ Jesus our Lord. (Rom. 8:38–39)

Your Father will never turn you away. The doors of this room are never closed. Learn to linger in the living room of God's house. When the words of others hurt you or your own failures distress you, step in here. Gaze at this painting and be reminded of your God: It is right to call him holy; we speak truth when we call him King. But if you want to touch his heart, use the name he loves to hear. Call him *Father*.

CHAPTER 3

THE FOUNDATION —Stability

WHERE TRUST BEGINS

Our Father who is . ○ —I am
He is

The most essential word in the Lord's Prayer is also the shortest. Be careful you don't miss it. A lot of people do. The word is so brief, it'll sneak right past you if you aren't careful.

Without it, the Great House of God cannot stand. Remove it and the house tumbles to the ground.

What is the word? I'll give you a hint. You just read it.

Where is it? You just read it.

Is it in this sentence? It is. It's also in the answer I just gave.

Come on, Max, is this a joke?

Would I kid you? (By the way, the word was in your question. See it?)

Is. "Our Father who *is* in heaven."

God is. Not God *was*. Not God *will be*. Not God *could be* or *should be*, but God *is*. He is the God of the present tense. And he is the foundation of his own house.

THE MORTAR OF FAITH

I write these words on an airplane. A late airplane. An airplane differ-ent from the one I was originally assigned. My first flight was canceled due to a mechanical difficulty. A few dozen not-so-happy campers and I were transferred to another plane. As we checked in for the new flight, I heard many of my fellow passengers ask the attendant, "Is this plane okay? Any mechanical flaws with this 747?" We were full of questions about the plane's ability to fly, but the ticket agent had no questions about our ability to do the same.

Not once were we asked, "How about you? Can you fly? Can you flap your arms and get airborne?" Of course, these are bizarre ques-tions. My ability to fly is not important. My strength is immaterial. I'm counting on the plane to get me home.

Need I make the connection? Your achievements, however noble they may be, are not important. Your credentials, as starry as they may be, are of no concern. God is the foundation of this house. The key question in life is not "How strong am I?" but rather "How strong is God?" Focus on his strength, not yours. Occupy yourself with the nature of God, not the size of your biceps.

That's what Moses did. Or at least that's what God told Moses to do. Remember the conversation at the burning bush? The tone was set in the first sentence. "Take off your sandals, because you are standing on holy ground" (Exod. 3:5). With these eleven words Moses is enrolled in a class on God. Immediately the roles are defined. God is holy. Approaching him on even a quarter-inch of leather is too pompous. And as we read further, we discover that no time is spent convincing Moses what Moses can do, but much time is spent explaining to Moses what God can do.

You and I tend to do the opposite. We would explain to Moses how he is ideally suited to return to Egypt. (Who better understands

His House built on boulders

the culture than a former prince?) Then we'd remind Moses how perfect he is for wilderness travel. (Who knows the desert better than
a shepherd?) We'd spend time reviewing with Moses his résumé and
strengths. (Come on, Moses, you can do it. Give it a try.)

But God doesn't. The strength of Moses is never considered. No
pep talk is given, no pats on the backs are offered. Not one word is
spoken to recruit Moses. But many words are used to reveal God. The
strength of Moses is not the issue; the strength of God is.

Shall we pause for application? Let's repeat that last sentence and
let you fill in a blank. Replace the name of Moses with your name.

The strength of _____ is not the issue; the strength of
God is.

You aren't the force behind the plane or the mortar within the
foundation; God is. I know you know that in your head, but do you
know that in your heart? Would you like to? Let me show you some of
the boulders that support this mighty house. Let me buttress your confidence in God's house by sharing with you some of his names.

WHAT'S IN A NAME?

Understanding the names of God is no quick study—after all, there
are more than eighty names for God in the Old Testament alone. But
if you want a place to begin, let me entice you with a few of the com-
pound names given God by some of the heroes of the faith. Each of
them reveals a different rock of God's character.

Maybe you are wondering how a study of the names of God can
help you understand him. Let me explain. Imagine that you and I are
having a conversation in 1978. You approach me on the college campus

where I was a student and ask, "Do you know Denalyn Preston?" I would have answered, "Let me think. Oh, I know Denalyn. She's an acquaintance of mine. She's that cute girl who likes to ride bikes and wear overalls to class." That's all I knew about her.

But go forward a year. Now we are in Miami, Florida, where I am a minister and Denalyn is a schoolteacher. "Do you know Denalyn Preston?" "Of course, I do. She's a friend. I see her every Sunday."

Ask me again a year later, "Denalyn Preston? Sure I know her. She can't take her eyes off of me." (Just kidding, honey.)

Fast-forward twelve months. "Who doesn't know Denalyn Preston?" I would answer. "You think she might be willing to go out on a date with me?"

Six months later, "Of course I know her—I can't quit thinking about her. We're going out again next week."

Two months later, "Do I know Denalyn Preston? I'm going to marry her next August!"

Now it's August of 1981. "Do I know Denalyn Preston? No, but I know Denalyn *Lucado*. She's my wife, and quit bugging us—we're on our honeymoon."

In three years my relationship with Denalyn evolved. And with each change came a new name. She went from *acquaintance* to *friend* to *eye-popping beauty* to *date* to *fiancée* and *wife*. Of course the names have only continued. Now she is *confidante, mother of my children, lifelong partner, boss* (just kidding, again). The more I know her, the more names I give her.

And the more God's people came to know him, the more names they gave him. Initially, God was known as *Elohim*. "In the beginning God [*Elohim*] created" (Gen. 1:1). The Hebrew word *Elohim* carries with it the meaning "strong one or creator" and appears thirty-one times in the first chapter of Genesis, where we see his creative power.[1]

As God revealed himself to his children, however, they saw him as more than a mighty force. They saw him as a loving Father who met them at every crossroad of their lives.   *The 1st big boulder*

Jacob, for example, came to see God as *Jehovah-raah*, a caring shepherd. "Like a shepherd," Jacob told his family, "God has led me all my life" (Gen. 48:15).

The phrase was surely a compliment to God, for Jacob was a less-than-cooperative sheep. Twice he tricked his brother, at least once he suckered his blind father. He out-crossed his double-crossing father-in-law by conning him out of his livestock and then, when the fellow wasn't looking, made like a Colt out of Baltimore in the middle of the night, sneaking off with anything that wasn't nailed down.

Jacob was never a candidate for the most well-behaved sheep award, but God never forgot him. He gave him food in the famine, forgiveness in his failures, and faith in his final years. Ask Jacob to describe God in a word, and his word would be *Jehovah-raah*, the caring shepherd.   *2nd*

Abraham had a different name for God: *Jehovah-jireh*, the Lord who provides. It's ironic that Abraham would call God "provider" since Abraham was well provided for already. He lived in a split-level tent with a four-camel garage. Life was good in Ur. "But life will be better in Canaan," he told his family. So off they went. When they asked, "Where will we live?" Abraham answered, "God will provide." And God did. When they got caught in an Egyptian scandal, the people wondered, "How will we get out?" Abraham assured them, "God will provide." And he did. When they split up the land and nephew Lot took the grassland and left Uncle Abraham with the rocks, the people wondered, "How will we survive?" Abraham knew the answer: "God will provide." And he did. And when Abraham and Sarah stood next to the empty crib and she wondered how he'd ever be the father of thousands, he'd put his arm around her, whispering, "The Lord will provide."

And God did. And Abraham bounced his firstborn on his hundred-year-old bony knees. Abraham learned that God provides. But even Abraham must have shaken his head when God asked him to sacrifice his own son on Mount Moriah.

Up the mountain they went. "Where is the lamb we will burn as a sacrifice?" his son asked (Gen. 22:7). One wonders how the answer made it past the lump in Abraham's throat: "God will give us the lamb for the sacrifice, my son" (v. 8). *Jehovah-jireh*, the Lord will provide. Abraham tied up his son and placed him on the altar and raised the knife, and the angel stayed his hand. Abraham had proven his faith. He heard a rustling in the thicket and saw a ram caught by his horns in a bush. He offered it as a sacrifice and gave the mountain a name, *Jehovah-jireh*, the Lord provides.

And then there is Gideon. The Lord came to Gideon and told him he was to lead his people in victory over the Midianites. That's like God telling a housewife to stand up to her abusive husband or a high school student to take on drug peddlers or a preacher to preach the truth to a congregation of Pharisees. "Y-y-you b-b-better get somebody else," we stammer. But then God reminds us that he knows we can't, but he can, and to prove it he gives a wonderful gift. He brings a spirit of peace. A peace before the storm. A peace beyond logic, or as Paul described it, a peace "which passes all understanding" (Phil. 4:7 RSV). He gave it to David after he showed him Goliath; he gave it to Saul after he showed him the gospel; he gave it to Jesus after he showed him the cross. And he gave it to Gideon. So Gideon, in turn, gave the name to God. He built an altar and named it *Jehovah-shalom*, the Lord is peace (Judg. 6:24).

At least a couple of the boulders beneath the house knew the chisel of Moses. On one he carved the name *Jehovah-rophe*. You'll find the English translation in Exodus 15:26: "I am the LORD who heals you." Here is the setting. Over a million Israelites have been liberated from captivity and now follow Moses into the desert. Their jubilation over liberation soon becomes frustration over dehydration. (Don't groan. I worked ten minutes on that sentence and fought two editors to keep it in.) They walked three days through a land void of shade, streams, houses, and greenery. Their only neighbors were the sun and serpents.

They finally came upon a lake, but the water was brackish, bitter, and dangerous. I'm sure it wasn't funny at the time, but you've got to chuckle about what happens next. "So Moses cried out to the LORD, and the LORD showed him a tree" (Exod. 15:25). Moses is begging for water and God gives him wood?

Let's pause and total the damage. Three days in the desert sun. Hopes raised at the sight of a lake. Hopes dashed at the taste of the water. Moses, cotton-mouthed and parched-lipped, asks for relief . . . and God shows him a tree?

Moses responds by throwing the tree into the lake. Maybe he did it out of aggravation: "Here is what I think of this tree stuff." Or maybe out of inspiration: "You're in charge, God." Whatever the reason, the water is purified, the Israelites' thirst is satisfied, and God is glorified. (That sentence only took five minutes.) In this case, God himself revealed his name: "I am the LORD who heals you" (Exod. 15:26).

The operative word here is *I.* God is the One who heals. He may use a branch of medicine and a branch of a hospital or a branch of a live oak tree, but he is the One who takes the poison out of the system. He is *Jehovah-rophe.*   *drug, alcohol, mind, soul.*

He is also *Jehovah-nissi,* the Lord my banner. In the heat of battle, soldiers feared getting separated from their army. For that reason a banner was carried into the conflict, and if a fighter found himself alone, the raised flag would signal safety. When the Amalekites (the big bad guys) attacked the Israelites (the little good guys), Moses went up on the mountain and prayed. As long as his hands were up, the Israelites prevailed. But when his hands were down, the Amalekites won. Moses was no dummy—he kept his hands up. The Israelites won, the Amalekites ran, and Moses built an altar for God and chiseled a new name on a stone—*Jehovah-nissi*—the Lord my banner (see Exod. 17:8–16).

These are just a few of the names of God that describe his character. Study them, for in a given day, you may need each one of them. Let me show you what I mean.

When you are confused about the future, go to your *Jehovah-raah*, your caring shepherd. When you are anxious about provision, talk to *Jehovah-jireh*, the Lord who provides. Are your challenges too great? Seek the help of *Jehovah-shalom*, the Lord is peace. Is your body sick? Are your emotions weak? *Jehovah-rophe*, the Lord who heals you, will see you now. Do you feel like a soldier stranded behind enemy lines? Take refuge in *Jehovah-nissi*, the Lord my banner.

Meditating on the names of God reminds you of the character of God. Take these names and bury them in your heart.

God is

the shepherd who guides,

the Lord who provides,

the voice who brings peace in the storm,

the physician who heals the sick, and

the banner that guides the soldier.

And most of all, he . . . is.

CHAPTER 4

THE OBSERVATORY

A HEAVENLY AFFECTION

Our Father who is in heaven . . .

A few mornings back I was jogging through my neighborhood. I've been known to miss some important dates, but even I could not miss the significance of that day. It was the first day of school. Reminders were everywhere: newscast interviews, stores packed with parents, yellow buses awakened from summer slumber and rumbling down the streets. My own family had spent the previous evening packing backpacks and preparing lunches.

It was no surprise to me, then, to see a pretty little girl step out of her house wearing new clothes and a backpack. She couldn't have been over five or six years of age and was walking toward the curb to wait for her bus. "Have a great first day of school," I greeted as I jogged past.

She stopped and looked at me as if I'd pulled a rabbit out of a hat. "How did you know?!"

She was stunned. From her perspective, I was a genius. Somehow I had miraculously discerned why she was up so early and where she was going. And she was impressed.

"Oh, I just know those kind of things," I shouted back to her. (No need to burst her bubble.)

You, on the other hand, are not so easily impressed. You know how I knew. You understand the difference between a child and a grown-up. Adults live in a different world than children. Remember how your parents amazed you? Remember how your dad could identify any car that passed? Weren't you impressed at your mom's ability to turn flour and milk and eggs into a cake? As my parents discussed the Sunday sermon, I can remember thinking, *I didn't understand a word the guy said.*

What's the difference? Simple. By virtue of training and study and experience, adults occupy a different domain. How much more is this true of God. Take the difference between the girl and me, amplify it a million times over, and we begin to see the contrast between us and our Father. Who among us can ponder God without asking the same question the girl did: How did you know?

We ask for grace, only to find forgiveness already offered. (How did you know I would sin?)

We ask for food, only to find provision already made. (How did you know I would be hungry?)

We ask for guidance, only to find answers in God's ancient story. (How did you know what I would ask?)

God dwells in a different realm. "The foolishness of God is wiser than human wisdom, and the weakness of God is stronger than human strength" (1 Cor. 1:25). He occupies another dimension. "My thoughts are not like your thoughts. Your ways are not like my ways. Just as the heavens are higher than the earth, so are my ways higher than your ways and my thoughts higher than your thoughts" (Isa. 55:8–9).

Make special note of the word *like.* God's thoughts are not our thoughts, nor are they even *like* ours. We aren't even in the same neighborhood. We're thinking, *Preserve the body*; he's thinking, *Save the soul.*

We dream of a pay raise. He dreams of raising the dead. We avoid pain and seek peace. God uses pain to bring peace. "I'm going to live before I die," we resolve. "Die, so you can live," he instructs. We love what rusts. He loves what endures. We rejoice at our successes. He rejoices at our confessions. We show our children the Nike star with the million-dollar smile and say, "Be like Mike." God points to the crucified carpenter with bloody lips and a torn side and says, "Be like Christ."

Our thoughts are not like God's thoughts. Our ways are not like his ways. He has a different agenda. He dwells in a different dimension. He lives on another plane. And that plane is named in the first phrase of the Lord's Prayer, "*Our Father who is in heaven.*"

THE OBSERVATORY

Having comforted us in the living room and assured us with the foundation, Jesus now leads us upstairs. We ascend to the highest level of the house, stand before a heavy wooden door, and accept God's invitation to enter his observatory.

No telescope is needed in this room. The glass ceiling magnifies the universe until you feel all of the sky is falling around you. Elevated instantly through the atmosphere, you are encircled by the heavens. Stars cascade past until you are dizzy with their number. Had you the ability to spend a minute on each planet and star, one lifetime would scarcely be enough to begin.

Jesus waits until you are caught up in the splendor of it all, and then he reminds you softly, "Your Father is in heaven."

I can remember as a youngster knowing some kids whose fathers were quite successful. One was a judge. The other a prominent physician. I attended church with the son of the mayor. In Andrews, Texas, that's not much to boast about. Nevertheless the kid had clout that most of us didn't. "My father has an office at the courthouse," he could claim.

Guess what you can claim? "My Father rules the universe."

> The heavens declare the glory of God, and the skies announce what his hands have made. Day after day they tell the story; night after night they tell it again. They have no speech or words; they have no voice to be heard. But their message goes out through all the world; their words go everywhere on earth. (Ps. 19:1–4)

Nature is God's workshop. The sky is his résumé. The universe is his calling card. You want to know who God is? See what he has done. You want to know his power? Take a look at his creation. Curious about his strength? Pay a visit to his home address: 1 Billion Starry Sky Avenue. Want to know his size? Step out into the night and stare at starlight emitted one million years ago and then read 2 Chronicles 2:6: "No one can really build a house for our God. Not even the highest of heavens can hold him."

He is untainted by the atmosphere of sin,
> unbridled by the timeline of history,
>> unhindered by the weariness of the body.

What controls you doesn't control him. What troubles you doesn't trouble him. What fatigues you doesn't fatigue him. Is an eagle disturbed by traffic? No, he rises above it. Is the whale perturbed by a hurricane? Of course not, he plunges beneath it. Is the lion flustered by the mouse standing directly in his way? No, he steps over it.

How much more is God able to soar above, plunge beneath, and step over the troubles of the earth! What is impossible with man is possible with God (Matt. 19:26). Our questions betray our lack of understanding:

How can God be everywhere at one time? (Who says God is bound by a body?)

How can God hear all the prayers that come to him? (Perhaps his ears are different from yours.)

How can God be the Father, the Son, and the Holy Spirit? (Could it be that heaven has a different set of physics than earth?)

If people down here won't forgive me, how much more am I guilty before a holy God? (Oh, just the opposite. God is always able to give grace when we humans can't—he invented it.)

How vital that we pray, armed with the knowledge that God is in heaven. Pray with any lesser conviction and your prayers are timid, shallow, and hollow. But spend some time walking in the workshop of the heavens, seeing what God has done, and watch how your prayers are energized.

Speaking of the Father's workshop, let me tell you about a visit I paid to one as an eight-year-old.

GOD'S WORKSHOP

The highlight of my Cub Scout career was the Soap Box Derby. You've heard of people standing on their soap boxes to make a point? We got *inside* our soap boxes to win a trophy. The competition was simple. Construct a motorless wooden go-cart and enter it in a downhill race. Some of the creations were fancy, complete with steering wheel and painted casing. Others were nothing more than a seat on a wooden chassis with four wheels and a rope for steering. My plan was to construct a genuine red roadster like the one in the Scout manual. Armed with a saw and hammer, a stack of lumber, and high ambition, I set out to be the Henry Ford of Troop 169.

I don't know how long my dad watched me before he interrupted my work. Probably not long, since my efforts weren't a pretty sight. The saw kept jamming and the wood kept buckling. The nails tended to bend and the panels didn't fit. At some point Dad mercifully intervened, tapped me on the shoulder, and told me to follow him into his workshop.

The small white frame house on the back of our lot was my dad's domain. I'd never really paid attention to what he did in there. All I knew was what I heard: buzzing saws, pounding hammers, and the whistle of a happy worker. I kept my bike in there, but I never noticed the tools. But then again, I'd never tried to build anything before. Over the next couple of hours that day, he introduced me to the magical world of sawhorses, squares, tape measures, and drills. He showed me how to draw a plan and measure the wood. He explained why it was wiser to hammer first and paint later. I was amazed. What was impossible for me was simple for him. Within an afternoon, we had constructed a pretty decent vehicle. And though I didn't leave the race with a trophy, I did leave with a greater admiration for my father. Why? I'd spent some time in his workshop.

You're following me on this one, aren't you? By showing us the heavens, Jesus is showing us his Father's workshop. He lets us hammer our thumbs just enough times and then taps us on the shoulder and says, "Your Father can handle that for you." And to prove it, he takes us into the Father's workshop. With a sweep of the hands he proudly proclaims: "Our Father is in heaven!"

Behold the sun! Every square yard of the sun is constantly emitting 130,000 horsepower, or the equivalent of 450 eight-cylinder automobile engines. And yet our sun, as powerful as it is, is but one minor star in the 100 billion orbs that make up our Milky Way Galaxy. Hold a dime in your fingers and extend it arm's length toward the sky, allowing it to eclipse your vision, and you will block out fifteen million stars from your view.

Consider the earth! Our globe's weight has been estimated at six sextillion tons (a six with twenty-one zeroes). Yet it is precisely tilted at twenty-three degrees; any more or any less and our seasons would be lost in a melted polar flood. Though our globe revolves at the rate of one thousand miles per hour or twenty-five thousand miles per day or nine million miles per year, none of us tumbles into orbit. Our God who "stretches the northern sky out over empty space and hangs the earth on nothing" (Job 26:7) also created an invisible band of gravity to hold us secure.[1]

Now as you stand in the observatory viewing God's workshop, let me pose a few questions. If he is able to place the stars in their sockets and suspend the sky like a curtain, do you think it remotely possible that God is able to guide your life? If your God is mighty enough to ignite the sun, could it be that he is mighty enough to light your path? If he cares enough about the planet Saturn to give it rings or Venus to make it sparkle, is there an outside chance that he cares enough about you to meet your needs? Or, as Jesus says,

> "Look at the birds in the air. They don't plant or harvest or store in barns, but your heavenly Father feeds them. And you know that you are worth much more than the birds. . . . And why do you worry about clothes? Look at how the lilies in the field grow. They don't work or make clothes for themselves. But I tell you that even Solomon with his riches was not dressed as beautifully as one of these flowers. God clothes the grass in the field, which is alive today but tomorrow is thrown into the fire. So you can be even more sure that God will clothe you. Don't have so little faith!" (Matt. 6:26–30)

Why did he do it? A shack would have sufficed, but he gave us a mansion. Did he have to give the birds a song and the mountains a peak? Was he required to put stripes on the zebra and the hump on the camel? Would we have known the difference had he made the sunsets gray instead of orange? Why do stars have twinkles and the waves snowy crests? Why dash the cardinal in red and drape the beluga whale in white? Why wrap creation in such splendor? Why go to such trouble to give such gifts?

Why do you? You do the same. I've seen you searching for a gift. I've seen you stalking the malls and walking the aisles. I'm not talking about the obligatory gifts. I'm not describing the last-minute purchase of drugstore perfume on the way to the birthday party. Forget blue-light specials and discount purchases; I'm talking about that extra-special person and that extra-special gift. I'm talking about stashing away a few dollars a month out of the grocery money to buy him some lizard-skin boots; staring at a thousand rings to find her the best diamond; staying up all night Christmas Eve, assembling the new bicycle. Why do you do it? You do it so the eyes will pop. You do it so the heart will stop. You do it so the jaw will drop. You do it to hear those words of disbelief, "You did this for me?"

That's why you do it. And that is why God did it. Next time a sunrise steals your breath or a meadow of flowers leaves you speechless, remain that way. Say nothing and listen as heaven whispers, "Do you like it? I did it just for you."

I'm about to tell you something you may find hard to believe. You're about to hear an opinion that may stretch your imagination. You don't have to agree with me, but I would like you to consider it with me. You don't have to buy it, but at least think about it. Here it is: *If you were the only person on earth, the earth would look exactly the same.* The Himalayas would still have their drama and the Caribbean would still have its charm. The sun would still nestle behind the Rockies in the evenings and spray light on the desert in the mornings. If you were the sole pilgrim on this globe, God would not diminish its beauty one degree.

Because he did it all for you . . . and he's waiting for you to discover his gift. He's waiting for you to stumble into the den, rub the sleep from your eyes, and see the bright red bike he assembled, just for you. He's waiting for your eyes to pop and your heart to stop. He's waiting for the moment between the dropping of the jaw and the leap of the heart. For in that silence he leans forward and whispers: *I did it just for you.*

Find such love hard to believe? That's okay. Remember the little girl who couldn't imagine how I knew she was going to school? Just because she couldn't comprehend it didn't mean I didn't know it. And just because we can't imagine God's giving us sunsets, don't think God doesn't do it. God's thoughts are higher than ours. God's ways are greater than ours. And sometimes, out of his great wisdom, our Father in heaven gives us a piece of heaven just to show he cares.

CHAPTER 5

THE CHAPEL

WHERE MAN COVERS HIS MOUTH

Hallowed be thy name . . .

When I lived in Brazil, I took my mom and her friend to see Iguaçú Falls, the largest waterfalls in the world. Some weeks earlier I'd become an expert on the cataracts by reading an article in *National Geographic* magazine. Surely, I thought, my guests would appreciate their good fortune in having me as a guide.

To reach the lookout point, tourists must walk a winding trail that leads them through a forest. I took advantage of the hike to give an Iguaçú nature report to my mom and her friend. So full of information I was, I chattered the entire time. After some minutes, however, I caught myself speaking louder and louder. A sound in the distance forced me to raise my voice. With each turn in the trail, my volume increased. Finally, I was shouting above a roar that was proving to be quite irritating. *Whatever that noise is, I wish they'd shut it off so I could complete my lecture.*

Only after reaching the clearing did I realize that the noise we heard was the waterfalls. My words were drowned out by the force and fury of what I was trying to describe. I could no longer be heard. Even if I could, I no longer had an audience. Even my mother would rather see the splendor than hear my description. I shut my mouth.

There are times when to speak is to violate the moment . . . when silence represents the highest respect. The word for such times is reverence. The prayer for such times is "Hallowed be thy name." And the place for this prayer is the chapel.

If there are walls, you won't notice them. If there is a pew, you won't need it. Your eyes will be fixed on God, and your knees will be on the floor. In the center of the room is a throne, and before the throne is a bench on which to kneel. Only you and God are here, and you can surmise who occupies the throne.

Don't worry about having the right words; worry more about having the right heart. It's not eloquence he seeks, just honesty.

A TIME TO BE SILENT

This was a lesson Job learned. If he had a fault, it was his tongue. He talked too much.

Not that anyone could blame him. Calamity had pounced on the man like a lioness on a herd of gazelles, and by the time the rampage passed, there was hardly a wall standing or a loved one living. Enemies had slaughtered Job's cattle, and lightning had destroyed his sheep. Strong winds had left his partying kids buried in wreckage.

And that was just the first day.

Job hadn't even had time to call Allstate before he saw the leprosy on his hands and the boils on his skin. His wife, compassionate soul that she was, told him to "curse God and die." His four friends came with the bedside manner of drill sergeants, telling him that God is fair and pain is the result of evil, and as sure as two-plus-two equals four, Job must have some criminal record in his past to suffer so.

Each had his own interpretation of God and each spoke long and loud about who God is and why God did what he did. They weren't the only ones talking about God. When his accusers paused, Job gave his response. Back and forth they went . . .

Job cried out . . . (3:1).

Then Eliphaz the Temanite answered . . . (4:1).

Then Job answered . . . (6:1).

Then Bildad the Shuhite answered . . . (8:1).

Then Job answered . . . (9:1).

Then Zophath the Naamathite answered . . . (11:1).

This verbal ping-pong continues for twenty-three chapters. Finally Job has enough of this "answering." No more discussion-group chitchat. It's time for the keynote address. He grips the microphone with one hand and the pulpit with the other and launches forth. For six chapters Job gives his opinions on God. This time the chapter headings read: "And Job continued," "And Job continued," "And Job continued." He defines God, explains God, and reviews God. One gets the impression that Job knows more about God than God does!

We are thirty-seven chapters into the book before God clears his throat to speak. Chapter thirty-eight begins with these words: "Then the LORD answered Job."

If your Bible is like mine, there is a mistake in this verse. The words are fine but the printer uses the wrong size type. The words should look like this:

THEN THE LORD ANSWERED JOB!

God speaks. Faces turn toward the sky. Winds bend the trees. Neighbors plunge into the storm shelters. Cats scurry up the trees and dogs duck into the bushes. "Somethin's a-blowin' in, honey. Best get them sheets off the line." God has no more than opened his mouth before Job knows he should have kept his sore one shut.

> "I will ask you questions, and you must answer me. Where were you when I made the earth's foundation? Tell me, if you understand. Who marked off how big it should be? Surely you know! Who stretched a ruler across it? What were the earth's foundations set on, or who put its cornerstone in place while the morning stars sang together and all the angels shouted with joy?" (38:3–7)

God floods the sky with queries, and Job cannot help but get the point: Only God defines God. You've got to know the alphabet before you can read, and God tells Job, "You don't even know the ABCs of heaven, much less the vocabulary." For the first time, Job is quiet. Silenced by a torrent of questions.

> "Have you ever gone to where the sea begins or walked in the valleys under the sea? Have you ever gone into the storehouse of the snow or seen the storehouses for hail . . . ?
>
> "Are you the one who gives the horse its strength or puts a flowing mane on its neck? Do you make the horse jump like a locust?

Is it through your wisdom that the hawk flies and spreads its wings toward the south?" (38:16, 22; 39:19–20, 26)

Job barely has time to shake his head at one question before he is asked another. The Father's implication is clear: "As soon as you are able to handle these simple matters of storing stars and stretching the neck of the ostrich, then we'll have a talk about pain and suffering. But until then, we can do without your commentary."

Does Job get the message? I think so. Listen to his response. "I am not worthy; I cannot answer you anything, so I will put my hand over my mouth" (40:4).

Notice the change. Before he heard God, Job couldn't speak enough. After he heard God, he couldn't speak at all.

Silence was the only proper response. There was a time in the life of Thomas à Kempis when he, too, covered his mouth. He had written profusely about the character of God. But one day God confronted him with such holy grace that, from that moment on, all à Kempis's words "seemed like straw." He put down his pen and never wrote another line. He put his hand over his mouth.

The word for such moments is reverence.

The room for such moments is the chapel.

The phrase for the chapel is "Hallowed be thy name."

A CUT ABOVE

This phrase is a petition, not a proclamation. A request, not an announcement. Hallowed *be* your name. We enter the chapel and beseech, "Be hallowed, Lord." Do whatever it takes to be holy in my life. Take your rightful place on the throne. Exalt yourself. Magnify yourself. Glorify yourself. You be Lord, and I'll be quiet.

The word *hallowed* comes from the word *holy*, and the word *holy* means "to separate." The ancestry of the term can be traced back to an ancient word that means "to cut." To be holy, then, is to be "a cut above" the norm, superior, extraordinary. Remember what we learned in the observatory? The holy One dwells on a different level from the rest of us. What frightens us does not frighten him. What troubles us does not trouble him.

I'm more a landlubber than a sailor, but I've puttered around in a bass boat enough to know the secret for finding land in a storm . . . You don't aim at another boat. You certainly don't stare at the waves. You set your sights on an object unaffected by the wind—a light on the shore—and go straight toward it. The light is unaffected by the storm.

By seeking God in the chapel, you do the same. When you set your sights on our God, you focus on One who is a cut above any storm life may bring.

Like Job, you find peace in the pain.

Like Job, you cover your mouth and sit still.

"Be still and know that I am God" (Ps. 46:10). This verse contains a command with a promise.

The command?

Be still.

Cover your mouth.

Bend your knees.

The promise? You will *know that I am God.*

The vessel of faith journeys on soft waters. Belief rides on the wings of waiting.

Linger in the chapel. Linger often in the chapel. In the midst of your daily storms, make it a point to be still and set your sights on him. Let God be God. Let him bathe you in his glory so that both your breath and your troubles are sucked from your soul. Be still. Be quiet. Be open and willing. Then you will know that God is God, and you can't help but confess, "Hallowed be thy name."

CHAPTER 6

THE THRONE

Thy kingdom come . . .

Our family went desk hunting recently. I needed a new one for the office, and we'd promised Andrea and Sara desks for their rooms. Sara was especially enthused. When she comes home from school, guess what she does? She plays school! I never did that as a kid. I tried to forget the classroom activities, not rehearse them. Denalyn assures me not to worry, that this is one of those attention-span differences between genders. So off to the furniture store we went.

When Denalyn buys furniture she prefers one of two extremes—so antique it's fragile or so new it's unpainted. This time we opted for the latter and entered a store of in-the-buff furniture.

Andrea and Sara succeeded quickly in making their selections, and I set out to do the same. Somewhere in the process Sara learned we weren't taking the desks home that day, and this news disturbed her deeply. I explained that the piece had to be painted first and would be delivered in about four weeks. I might as well have said four millennia. Her eyes filled with tears. "But, Daddy, I wanted to take it home today."

Much to her credit she didn't stomp her feet and demand her way. She did, however, set out on an urgent course to change her father's mind. Every time I turned a corner she was waiting on me.

"Daddy, don't you think we could paint it ourselves?"

"Daddy, I just want to draw some pictures on my new desk."

"Daddy, please let's take it home today."

After a bit she disappeared, only to return, arms open wide and bubbling with a discovery. "Guess what, Daddy. It'll fit in the back of the car!"

You and I know that a seven-year-old has no clue what will or won't fit in a vehicle, but the fact that she had measured the trunk with her arms softened my heart. The clincher, though, was the name she called me: "Daddy, can't we please take it home?"

The Lucado family took a desk home that day.

I heard Sara's request for the same reason God hears ours. Her desire was for her own good. What dad wouldn't want his child to spend more time writing and drawing? Sara wanted what I wanted for her, she only wanted it sooner. When we agree with what God wants, he hears us as well. (See 1 John 5:14.)

Sara's request was heartfelt. God, too, is moved by our sincerity. The "earnest prayer of a righteous man has great power" (James 5:16 TLB).

But most of all, I was moved to respond because Sara called me "Daddy." Because she is my child, I heard her request. Because we are his children, God hears ours. The King of creation gives special heed to the voice of his family. He is not only willing to hear us, he loves to hear us. He even tells us what to ask him.

"Thy kingdom come."

THY KINGDOM COME

We're often content to ask for less. We entered the Great House of God with a satchel full of requests—promotions desired, pay raises wanted, transmission repairs needed, and tuitions due. We'd typically say our prayers as casually as we'd order a burger at the drive-through: "I'll have one solved problem and two blessings, cut the hassles, please."

But such complacency seems inappropriate in the chapel of worship. Here we are before the King of kings. We've just covered our mouths out of reverence for his holiness, now do we open them with the topic of transmissions? Not that our needs don't matter to him, mind you. It's just that what seemed so urgent outside the house seems less significant in here. The pay raise is still needed, and the promotion is still desired, but is that where we start?

Jesus tells how to begin. "When you pray, pray like this. 'Our Father who is in heaven, hallowed be thy name. Thy kingdom come.'"

When you say, "Thy kingdom come," you are inviting the Messiah himself to walk into your world. "Come, my King! Take your throne in our land. Be present in my heart. Be present in my office. Come into my marriage. Be Lord of my family, my fears, and my doubts." This is no feeble request; it's a bold appeal for God to occupy every corner of your life.

Who are you to ask such a thing? Who are you to ask God to take control of your world? You are his child, for heaven's sake! And so you ask boldly. "Let us then with confidence draw near to the throne of grace, that we may receive mercy and find grace to help in time of need" (Heb. 4:16 RSV).

A SPIRITUAL DRAMA

A wonderful illustration of this kind of boldness is in the story of Hadassah. Though her language and culture are an atlas apart from ours, she can tell you about the power of a prayer to a king. There are a couple of differences, though. Her request was not to her father but to her husband, the king. Her prayer wasn't for a desk but for the delivery of her people. And because she entered the throne room, because she opened her heart to the king, he changed his plans and millions of people in 127 different countries were saved.

Oh, how I'd love for you to meet Hadassah. But since she lived in the fifth century BC, such an encounter is not likely. We'll have to be content with reading about her in the book that bears her name—her other name—the book of Esther.

And what a book it is! Hollywood would have a challenge matching the drama of this story . . . the evil Haman who demanded that all pay him homage . . . the gutsy Mordecai who refused to bow before Haman . . . Mordecai's great words to Esther that she may have been chosen queen for "such a time as this" . . . and Esther's conviction to save her people. "If I perish, I perish," she resolved.

Let's review the central characters.

Xerxes was the king of Persia. He was an absolute monarch over the land from India to Ethiopia. Let Xerxes raise an eyebrow and the destiny of the world would change. In this respect he symbolized the power of God, for our King guides the river of life, and he doesn't even raise an eyebrow.

Haman (whose name sounds like hangman, which you will soon see as more than a curious coincidence) was the right-hand man of Xerxes. Read every word about the man and you'll find nothing good about him. He was an insatiable egotist who wanted the worship of every person in the kingdom. Perturbed by a peculiar minority called the Jews, he decided to exterminate them. He convinced Xerxes that the world would be better with a holocaust and set a date for the genocide of all of Abraham's children.

Haman is a servant of hell and a picture of the devil himself, who has no higher aim than to have every knee bow as he passes. Satan also has no other plan than to persecute the promised people of God. He "comes to steal and kill and destroy" (John 10:10). "He is filled with anger, because he knows he does not have much time" (Rev. 12:12). Since the lie in the garden, he has sought to derail God's plan. In this case Satan hopes to destroy the Jews, thereby destroying the lineage of Jesus. For Haman, the massacre is a matter of expediency. For Satan, it is a matter of survival. He will do whatever it takes to impede the presence of Jesus in the world.

That's why he doesn't want you to pray as Jesus taught, "Thy kingdom come."

Esther, Mordecai's adopted daughter, became queen by winning a Miss Persia contest. In one day she went from obscurity to royalty, and in more ways than one she reminds you of you. Both of you are residents of the palace: Esther, the bride of Xerxes, and you, the bride of Christ. Both of you have access to the throne of the king, and you both have a counselor to guide and teach you. Your counselor is the Holy Spirit. Esther's counselor was Mordecai.

It was Mordecai who urged Esther to keep her Jewish nationality a secret. It was also Mordecai who persuaded Esther to talk to Xerxes about the impending massacre. You may wonder why she would need any encouragement. Mordecai must have wondered the same thing. Listen to the message he got from Esther: "No man or woman may go to the king in the inner courtyard without being called. There is only one law about this: Anyone who enters must be put to death unless the king holds out his gold scepter. Then that person may live. And I have not been called to go to the king for thirty days" (Est. 4:11).

As strange as it may sound to us, not even the queen could approach the king without an invitation. To enter his throne room uninvited was to risk a visit to the gallows. But Mordecai convinced her to take the risk. If you wonder why I see Mordecai as a picture of the Holy Spirit, watch how he encouraged her to do what is right. "Just because you live in the king's palace, don't think that out of all the Jewish people you alone will escape. If you keep quiet at this time, someone else will help and save the Jewish people, but you and your father's family will all die. And who knows, you may have been chosen queen for just such a time as this" (Est. 4:13–14).

Watch how Esther responded. "Esther put on her royal robes and stood in the inner courtyard of the king's palace, facing the king's hall" (Est. 5:1).

Can't you see her? Right off the cover of *Mademoiselle* magazine? Can't you see King Xerxes? Flipping through his copy of *Car and Chariot*. On either side of him is a burly-chested guard. Behind him is a chattering eunuch. Ahead of him is a long day of cabinet meetings and royal red tape. He lets out a sigh and sinks down into his throne . . . and out of the corner of his eye, he sees Esther.

"When the king saw Queen Esther standing in the courtyard, he was pleased" (5:2). Let me give you my translation of that verse: "When the king saw Queen Esther standing in the courtyard he said, 'a-hubba-hubba-hubba.'" "He held out to her the gold scepter that was in his hand, so Esther went forward and touched the end of it" (5:2).

What follows is the rapid collapse of Satan's deck of cards. Haman schemes to string up Mordecai, the only man who won't grovel at his feet. Esther plans to throw a couple of banquets for Xerxes and Haman. At the end of the second banquet Xerxes begs Esther to ask for something. Esther looks sort of sheepishly at the floor and says, "Well, now that you mention it, there is one eensy-weensy favor I've been wanting to ask." And she proceeds to inform the king about the raging anti-Semite who was hell-bent on killing her friends like rats, which meant that Xerxes was about to lose his bride if he didn't act soon, and you don't want that, do you, honey?

Xerxes demands the name of the murderer, and Haman looks for the exits. Esther spills the beans, and Xerxes loses his cool. He storms out the door to take a Prozac only to return and find Haman at the feet of Esther. Haman is begging for mercy, but the king thinks he's making a move on the queen. And before Haman has a chance to explain, he's headed to the same gallows he'd built for Mordecai.

Haman gets Mordecai's rope. Mordecai gets Haman's job. Esther gets a good night's sleep. The Jews live to see another day. And we get a dramatic reminder of what happens when we approach our King.

Like Esther, we have been plucked out of obscurity and given a place in the palace.

Like Esther, we have royal robes; she was dressed in cloth, we are dressed in righteousness.

Like Esther, we have the privilege of making our request.

That's what Sara did. Her request wasn't as dramatic as Esther's, but it changed her father's plans. By the way, the living parable of Sara and her desk didn't stop at the store.

On the way home she realized that my desk was still at the store. "I guess you didn't beg, did you, Daddy?" (We have not because we ask not.)

When we unloaded her desk, she invited me to christen it with her by drawing a picture. I made a sign that read, "Sara's desk." She made a sign that read, "I love my Daddy." (Worship is the right response to answered prayer.)

My favorite part of the story is what happened the next day. I shared this account in my Sunday sermon. A couple from our church dropped by and picked up the desk, telling us they would paint it. When they returned it a couple of days later, it was covered with angels. And I was reminded that when we pray for God's kingdom to come, it comes! All the hosts of heaven rush to our aid.

CHAPTER 7

THE STUDY

HOW GOD REVEALS HIS WILL

Thy will be done . . .

Were the scene not so common it would be comical. Two heavyhearted disciples slouching their way home to Emmaus. By the slump in their shoulders, you'd never know today was Resurrection Sunday. By the looks on their faces, you'd think Jesus was still in the tomb. "We were hoping that he would free Israel," they lamented (Luke 24:21).

As if he hasn't! How could you be so close to Christ and miss the point? Jesus has just redeemed the world and they are complaining about Rome? Jesus came to deal with sin and death—and they want him to deal with Caesar and soldiers? Jesus came to set us free from hell—and they want to be set free from taxes?

Talk about a miscommunication! They missed the revolution!

I made the same mistake last month. The revolution I missed was nothing like the ones the disciples missed, but I missed it just the same.

The New England colonies were never the same after the Boston Tea Party. Europe was never the same after the Battle of Normandy.

The church was never the same after Luther hammered his ninety-five theses on the Wittenburg Door. And my life has never been the same since e-mail entered our office.

The avant-garde thinkers on the church staff had been lobbying for this change for months. "Just think," they would say, "just move the cursor and click the mouse, and the message is sent."

Easy for them to say. They speak Computer-ese. Not me. Up until recently I thought a cursor was a person with foul language and a mouse was a rodent you trapped. As far as I knew, logging-on was the job of the lumberjack, and a monitor was the guy who asked you what you were doing roaming the halls during class.

How was I to know that *interface* was a computer term? I thought it was slang for a slam dunk. (Interface, baby!) Forgive me for lagging behind (or is that "logging behind"?), but a fellow can only handle so much. It happened overnight. I went to sleep in a simple society of sticky notes and awoke in a paperless culture of e-mail. You can imagine my confusion as everyone started jabbering in this new vocabulary: "I e-mailed you a memo I found at www.confusion.com." "Why don't you download your bat.file in my subdirectory, and we can interface on the Internet?"

What was wrong with, "Did you get my note?"

I miss the old days. I miss the bygone era of pen touching paper and sticky notes on my door. I long to see handwriting again and to use the "while you were out message" as a coaster for my coffee cup.

But change was inevitable and, digging my heels in the carpet, I was pulled into the netherworld of e-mail. Partly because I was busy but mostly because I was stubborn, I procrastinated learning the system. Every day the computer net mail beeped to alert me about incoming messages. And every day the number increased. "Max Lucado has 10 unread messages in his box." "Max Lucado has 52 unread messages in his box." "Max Lucado has 93 unread messages in his box."

Finally I gave in. After being carefully tutored and mastering the correct double-click of the hamster (I mean the mouse), I found myself gazing inside a room full of information, all waiting for me. There was a letter from Africa, a joke about preachers, a dozen or so announcements about meetings (I had missed—oops!). Within a few minutes I was updated, informed, and, I'll admit it, enlightened. As much as I hate to say so, it felt good to get the messages again.

Which is similar to how the two men on the road to Emmaus must have felt. They, too, had missed out on some information. They, too, were confused. They'd missed more than a memo on a committee meeting, however. They'd missed the meaning of the death of Jesus. What should have been a day of joy was to them a day of despair. Why? They didn't know how to understand God's will.

They aren't alone. More than one of us has spent hours staring at the monitor of life wondering what direction to take. We know God has a will for us. "I have good plans for you, not plans to hurt you. I will give you hope and a good future" (Jer. 29:11).

God has a plan, and that plan is good. Our initial question is, how do I access it? Other people seem to receive guidance; how can I? One of the best ways to answer these questions is to study the story of these two confused disciples on the road to Emmaus. And I know no better time than now to answer the questions as we enter into the next room in God's Great House and pray, "Thy will be done."

Study what his will is for us.

THE STUDY

Just down the hall from the chapel is a room uncluttered by televisions, stereos, and e-mail-infected computers. Envision a study with bookshelves lining the walls, a braided rug on the floor, and an inviting fire in the hearth. In front of the fire are two high, wing chairs, one for you and one for your Father. Your seat is empty, and your Father motions for you to join him. Come and sit and ask him whatever is on your heart. No question is too small, no riddle too simple. He has all the time in the world. Come and seek the will of God.

To pray, "Thy will be done" is to seek the heart of God. The word *will* means "strong desire." The study is where we learn what God desires. What is his heart? His passion? He wants you to know it.

Shall God hide from us what he is going to do? Apparently not, for he has gone to great lengths to reveal his will to us. Could he have done more than send his Son to lead us? Could he have done more than give his word to teach us? Could he have done more than orchestrate events to awaken us? Could he have done more than send his Holy Spirit to counsel us?

God is not the God of confusion, and wherever he sees sincere seekers with confused hearts, you can bet your sweet December that he will do whatever it takes to help them see his will. That's what he was doing on the road to Emmaus.

Everybody else was online, and they were on foot. They saw the death of Jesus as the death of the movement, and they packed their bags and headed home. And that is where they were going when Jesus appeared to them. How sweet is the appearance of Jesus on the road. Let a lamb take the wrong turn and miss the pasture, and our Shepherd, unwilling to let him wander too far, comes to guide him home. How does he do this? How does he reveal his will to us? You might be surprised at the simplicity of the process.

THROUGH THE PEOPLE OF GOD

The first mistake of the duo was to disregard the words of their fellow disciples. God reveals his will through a community of believers. On the first Easter, he spoke through women who spoke to the others. "Today some women among us amazed us. Early this morning they went to the tomb, but they did not find his body there. They came and told us that they had seen a vision of angels who said that Jesus was alive!" (Luke 24:22–23).

His plan hasn't changed. Jesus still speaks to believers through believers. "The whole body depends on Christ, and all the parts of the body are joined and held together. Each part does its own work to make the whole body grow and be strong with love" (Eph. 4:16).

While I was driving to my office this morning, my eye saw a traffic light. The sensors within my eye perceived that the color of the light was red. My brain checked my memory bank and announced the meaning of a red light to my right foot. My right foot responded by leaving the accelerator and pressing the brake.

Now what if my body hadn't functioned properly? What if my eye had decided not to be a part of the body because the nose had hurt its feelings? Or what if the foot was tired of being bossed around and decided to press the gas pedal instead of the brake? Or what if the right foot was in pain but too proud to tell the left foot, so the left foot didn't know to step in and help? In all instances, a wreck would occur.

God has given each part of the body of Christ an assignment. One way God reveals his will to you is through the church. He speaks to one member of his body through another member. It could happen in a Bible class, a small group, during communion, or during dessert. God has as many methods as he has people.

That, by the way, is why Satan doesn't want you in church. You've noticed, haven't you, that when you're in a spiritual slump, you head out to Emmaus too. You don't want to be with believers. Or if you do, you sneak in and sneak out of the service, making excuses about meals to prepare or work to do. The truth is, Satan doesn't want you hearing God's will. And since God reveals his will to his children through other children, Satan doesn't want you in a church. Nor does he want you reading your Bible. Which takes us to another way God reveals his will.

THROUGH THE WORD OF GOD

The disciples disregarded the Word of God. That was their second mistake. Rather than consult the Scriptures, they listened to their fears. Jesus corrects this by appearing to them and conducting a Bible study. We'd expect something a bit more dramatic from one who had just defeated death—turn a tree into a dog or suspend the disciples a few feet in the air. But Jesus sees no need to do more than reacquaint his followers with Scripture.

> "You are foolish and slow to believe everything the prophets said. They said that the Christ must suffer these things before he enters his glory." Then starting with what Moses and the prophets had said about him, Jesus began to explain everything that had been written about himself in the Scriptures. (Luke 24:25–27)

Through the words of the prophets, he used Scripture to reveal his will. Doesn't he do the same today? Open the Word of God and you'll find his will.

> "This is the will of the Father . . . that of all He has given Me I should lose nothing, but should raise it up." (John 6:39 NKJV)

> It is God's will that you be born again, that you be born not "of the will of the flesh, nor of the will of man, but of God." (John 1:13 NKJV)

> It is not God's will that one little one perish. (Matt. 18:14)

"This is the will of my Father, that every one who sees the Son and believes in him should have eternal life, and I will raise him up at the last day." (John. 6:40 RSV)

It is his will that the world be saved. Knowing that, then, my task is to align myself with his will. Anytime I find myself choosing between two roads I must ask, "Which road will contribute more to the kingdom of God?"

Sometimes it's obvious. There is no way, for example, that pornography advances the cause of God. It's beyond reason to think that embezzlement enhances the kingdom (even if you tithe on your take). I would take issue with the person who justifies her drug addiction as a way to draw nearer to the mystical side of God.

Other times it's not as clear, but the question is still helpful. Forced to choose between two professions? Will one allow you to have a greater impact for the kingdom? Torn between two churches to attend? Will one afford you a greater chance to glorify God? You wonder if this person is the spouse for you? Ask yourself, will he or she help me bring glory to God?

His *general* will provides us with guidelines that help us understand his *specific* will for our individual lives.

Through a Walk with God

They begged him, "Stay with us; . . . it is almost night." So he went in to stay with them. (Luke 24:29)

We also learn God's will by spending time in his presence. The key to knowing God's heart is having a relationship with him. A *personal* relationship. God will speak to you differently than he will speak to others. Just because God spoke to Moses through a burning bush, that doesn't mean we should all sit next to a bush waiting for God to speak. God used a fish to convict Jonah. Does that mean we should have worship services at Sea World? No. God reveals his heart personally to each person.

For that reason, your walk with God is essential. His heart is not seen in an occasional chat or weekly visit. We learn his will as we take up residence in his house every single day.

If you were to take a name at random out of the phone book and ask me, "Max, how does Chester Whomever feel about adultery?" I couldn't answer. I don't know Chester Whomever. But if you were to ask me, "Max, how does Denalyn Lucado feel about adultery?" I wouldn't even have to call her. I know. She's my wife. We have walked together long enough that I know what she thinks.

The same is true with God. Walk with him long enough and you come to know his heart. When you spend time with him in his study, you see his passion. Welcome him to enter the gateway of your soul and you'll perceive his will. By the way, did you notice that curious action of Jesus found in verse 28? "They came near the town of Emmaus, and Jesus acted as if he were going farther."

Doesn't Jesus want to be with the disciples? Of course he does. But he doesn't want to be where he's not invited. Ever the gentleman, our Lord awaits our invitation. Please note, it was after they gave this invitation that "they were allowed to recognize Jesus" (v. 31).

There is one final way God reveals his will.

THROUGH THE FIRE OF GOD

When they saw who he was, he disappeared.

They said to each other, "It felt like a fire burning in us when

Jesus talked to us on the road and explained the Scriptures to us."
(Luke 24:31–32)

Don't you love that verse? They knew they had been with Jesus because of the fire within them. God reveals his will by setting a torch to your soul. He gave Jeremiah a fire for hard hearts. He gave Nehemiah a fire for a forgotten city. He set Abraham on fire for a land he'd never seen. He set Isaiah on fire with a vision he couldn't resist. Forty years of fruitless preaching didn't extinguish the fire of Noah. Forty years of wilderness wandering didn't douse the passion of Moses. Jericho couldn't slow Joshua, and Goliath didn't deter David. There was a fire within them.

And isn't there one within you? Want to know God's will for your life? Then answer this question: What ignites your heart? Forgotten orphans? Untouched nations? The inner city? The outer limits?

Heed the fire within!

Do you have a passion to sing? Then sing!

Are you stirred to manage? Then manage!

Do you ache for the ill? Then treat them!

Do you hurt for the lost? Then teach them!

As a young man I felt the call to preach. Unsure if I was correct in my reading of God's will for me, I sought the counsel of a minister I admired. His counsel still rings true. "Don't preach," he said, "unless you have to."

As I pondered his words I found my answer: "I *have* to. If I don't, the fire will consume me."

What is the fire that consumes you?

Mark it down: Jesus comes to set you on fire! He walks as a torch from heart to heart, warming the cold and thawing the chilled and stirring the ashes. He is at once a Galilean wildfire and a welcome candle. He comes to purge infection and illuminate your direction.

The fire of your heart is the light of your path. Disregard it at your own expense. Fan it at your own delight. Blow it. Stir it. Nourish it. Cynics will doubt it. Those without it will mock it. But those who know it—those who know *him*—will understand it.

To meet the Savior is to be set aflame.

To discover the flame is to discover his will.

And to discover his will is to access a world like none you've ever seen.

CHAPTER 8

THE FURNACE

BECAUSE SOMEONE PRAYED

In earth, as it is in heaven . . .

I'd like you to think about someone. His name is not important. His looks are immaterial. His gender is of no concern. His title is irrelevant. He is important not because of who he is but because of what he did.

He went to Jesus on behalf of a friend. His friend was sick, and Jesus could help, and someone needed to go to Jesus, so someone went. Others cared for the sick man in other ways. Some brought food; others provided treatment; still others comforted the family. Each role was crucial. Each person was helpful, but none was more vital than the one who went to Jesus.

He went because he was asked to go. An earnest appeal came from the family of the afflicted. "We need someone who will tell Jesus that my brother is sick. We need someone to ask him to come. Will you go?"

The question came from two sisters. They would have gone themselves, but they couldn't leave their brother's bedside. They needed someone else to go for them. Not just anyone, mind you, for not just anyone could. Some were too busy; others didn't know the way. Some fatigued too quickly; others were inexperienced on the path. Not everyone could go.

And not everyone would go. This was no small request the sisters were making. They needed a diligent ambassador, someone who knew how to find Jesus. Someone who wouldn't quit mid-journey. Someone who would make sure the message was delivered. Someone who was as convinced as they were that Jesus *must* know what had happened.

They knew of a trustworthy person, and to that person they went. They entrusted their needs to someone, and that someone took those needs to Christ.

"So Mary and Martha sent *someone* to tell Jesus, 'Lord, the one you love is sick'" (John 11:3, emphasis mine).

Someone carried the request. Someone walked the trail. Someone went to Jesus on behalf of Lazarus. And because someone went, Jesus responded.

Let me ask you, how important was this person in the healing of Lazarus? How essential was his role? Some might regard it as secondary. After all, didn't Jesus know everything? Certainly he knew that Lazarus was sick. Granted, but he didn't respond to the need until someone came to him with the message. "When Jesus heard this, he said, 'This sickness will not end in death. It is for the glory of God, to bring glory to the Son of God'" (v. 4).

When was Lazarus healed? After *someone* made the request. Oh, I know the healing wouldn't unfold for several days, but the timer was set when the appeal was made. All that was needed was the passage of time.

Would Jesus have responded if the messenger had not spoken? Perhaps, but we have no guarantee. We do, however, have an example: The power of God was triggered by prayer. Jesus looked down the very throat of death's cavern and called Lazarus back to life . . . all because someone prayed.

THE FURNACE

In the Great House of God there is a furnace. This furnace affects the whole house, and your prayers fuel the furnace. Your intercession is coal on the fire. Your pleadings are kindling to the flames. The furnace is sturdy, and the vents are ready; all that is needed is your prayer.

> Prayer is essential in this ongoing warfare. Pray hard and long. Pray
> for your brothers and sisters. (Eph. 6:18 MSG)

In the economy of heaven, the prayers of saints are a valued commodity. John, the apostle, would agree. He wrote the story of Lazarus and was careful to show the sequence: The healing began when the request was made.

This wouldn't be the last time John would make the same point. Read these words, penned later by John. "On the Lord's day I was in the Spirit, and I heard a loud voice behind me that sounded like a trumpet" (Rev. 1:10).

IN THE SPIRIT ON THE LORD'S DAY

We've just moved six decades into the future. John is old now. He's the silver-haired figure stepping through the jagged rocks on a beach. He's looking for a flat place where he can kneel. It is the Lord's Day. And John has come to see his Lord.

We don't know who first called this day the Lord's Day, but we know why. It was and is his day. It belongs to him. He left his imprint on hell itself that morning. Friday's trial became Sunday's trumpet. This is the Lord's Day.

This is also John's spiritual birthday. Decades earlier, on the first Lord's Day, John was shaken from his sorrow and sleep by the announcement, "They have taken the Lord out of the tomb, and we don't know where they have put him" (John 20:2). On legs much younger and stronger, John sprinted to the empty tomb and the fulfilled promise. Speaking of himself, he later confided, "Then the other follower, who had reached the tomb first, also went in. He saw and believed" (John 20:8).

After the resurrection came persecution, and the Father scattered his disciples over society like a spring wind scatters dandelions. John, the eyewitness, was placed in Ephesus. There is good reason to believe he spent every Lord's Day in the same way he spent the first, leading a friend into the empty tomb of Jesus.

But on this Sunday he has no friend to take to the tomb. He is exiled, banished from his friends. Alone on Patmos. Cut off. With the stroke of a magistrate's pen, he was sentenced to pass his days with no companion, with no church.

Rome had stilled the tongue of Peter and silenced the pen of Paul. Now she would break the shepherd's staff of John. No doubt she felt smug in her proscription. One by one, the iron fist of Caesar would crush the fragile work of the Galilean.

If only she had known. But she had no idea. No clue. No concept. For what Rome intended as isolation, heaven ordained as revelation. Rome placed John on Patmos for punishment. Heaven placed John on Patmos for privilege. The same apostle who saw the open grave of Christ was now to glimpse the open door of heaven.

It was the Lord's Day, you see. Nothing Rome could do could change that fact. It was the Lord's Day in Rome and in Jerusalem. It was the Lord's Day in Egypt and Ethiopia and even along the barren stretches of Patmos. It was the Lord's Day. And John was, in his words, "in the Spirit" on the Lord's Day. Though he was cut off from man, he was in the very presence of God. Though he was far from friends, he was face-to-face with his Friend. He was praying.

And as he prayed, he again was met by an angel. He again saw what no man had ever seen. The same eyes that saw the resurrected Lord now saw heaven open. And for the next few seconds, minutes, or days, John was caught up in the fury and passion of living in the end of times and in the presence of God.

AND HEAVEN WAS SILENT

Though much could be said about what he saw, let's focus on what he heard. Before John speaks of what he saw, he speaks of what he heard, and what he heard was stunning. "On the Lord's day I was in the Spirit, and I heard a loud voice behind me that sounded like a trumpet" (Rev. 1:10). I can imagine a voice, and I can imagine a trumpet, but to imagine the silver-toned trumpet-voice, is beyond me. And so we are welcomed to the world of Revelation, a realm where what can't happen on earth always happens in heaven.

For eight chapters we read about the noises of heaven John's ears hear—the glorious, loud, rambunctious, soft, holy sounds of heaven. The angels speak. The thunder booms. The living creatures chant, "Holy, holy, holy" (4:8) and the elders worship, "You are worthy, our Lord and God, to receive glory and honor and power, because you made all things" (4:11). The souls of the martyrs call out, "How long?" (6:10). The earth quakes, and the stars fall like figs in a windstorm. One hundred forty-four thousand people from every nation, tribe, people, and language of the earth shout in a loud voice, "Salvation belongs to our God, who sits on the throne, and to the Lamb" (7:10).

The air is full of sounds—earthquakes, trumpets, proclamations, and declarations. From the first word of the angel there is constant activity and nonstop noise until: "there was silence in heaven for about half an hour" (8:1). Strange this sudden reference to minutes.

Nothing else is timed. We are not told the length of the worship or the duration of the songs, but the silence lasted for "about half an hour." "What do you mean, 'about half an hour'?" we want to ask. Did John time it? Why "half an hour"? Why not fifteen minutes or one hour? I don't know. I don't know if John was literal or symbolic. But I do know that, as an orchestra falls silent at the lifting of the conductor's baton, so heaven hushed when the Lamb opened the seventh seal.

As the first six seals revealed how God acts, the seventh revealed how God listens. Look what happens after the seventh seal is opened.

> When the Lamb opened the seventh seal, there was silence in heaven for about half an hour. And I saw the seven angels who stand before God and to whom were given seven trumpets. Another angel came and stood at the altar, holding a golden pan for incense. He was given much incense to offer with the prayers of all God's holy people. The angel put this offering on the golden altar before the throne. The smoke from the incense went up from the angel's hand to God with the prayers of God's people. Then the angel filled the incense pan with fire from the altar and threw it on the earth, and there were flashes of lightning, thunder and loud noises, and an earthquake. (8:1–5)

Every song ceased. Every being of the heavenly city hushed. The noise stopped. A sudden stillness fell like a curtain. Why? Why did the Lamb lift his hand for silence? Why did the silver-trumpet voices hush? Because someone was praying. Heaven paused, and heaven pauses to hear the prayers of . . . someone. A mother for her child. A pastor for a church. A doctor for the diseased. A counselor for the confused. Someone steps up to the furnace with a burden and prays, "Lord, the one you love is sick."

WHEN JESUS HEARD THIS

The phrase the friend of Lazarus used is worth noting. When he told Jesus of the illness he said, "Lord, the one you love is sick." He doesn't base his appeal on the imperfect love of the one in need but on the perfect love of the Savior. He doesn't say, "The one *who loves you* is sick." He says, "The one *you love* is sick." The power of the prayer, in other words, does not depend on the one who makes the prayer but on the One who hears the prayer.

We can and must repeat the phrase in manifold ways. "The one you love is tired, sad, hungry, lonely, fearful, depressed." The words of the prayer vary, but the response never changes. The Savior hears the prayer. He silences heaven, so he won't miss a word. He hears the prayer. Remember the phrase from John's gospel? "When Jesus *heard* this, he said, 'This sickness will not end in death'" (John 11:4, emphasis mine).

The Master heard the request. Jesus stopped whatever he was doing and took note of the man's words. This anonymous courier was heard by God.

You and I live in a loud world. To get someone's attention is no easy task. He must be willing to set everything aside to listen: turn down the radio, turn away from the monitor, turn the corner of the page and set down the book. When someone is willing to silence everything else so he can hear us clearly, it is a privilege. A rare privilege, indeed.

So John's message is critical. You can talk to God because God listens. Your voice matters in heaven. He takes you very seriously. When you enter his presence, the attendants turn to you to hear your voice. No need to fear that you will be ignored. Even if you stammer or stumble, even if what you have to say impresses no one, it impresses God—and he listens. He listens to the painful plea of the elderly in the rest home. He listens to the gruff confession of the death-row inmate. When the alcoholic begs for mercy, when the spouse seeks guidance, when the businessman steps off the street into the chapel, God listens.

Intently. Carefully. The prayers are honored as precious jewels. Purified and empowered, the words rise in a delightful fragrance to our Lord. "The smoke from the incense went up from the angel's hand to God" (Rev. 8:4). Incredible. Your words do not stop until they reach the very throne of God.

"Then the angel filled the incense pan with fire from the altar and threw it on the earth" (v. 5). One call and Heaven's fleet appears. Your prayer on earth activates God's power in heaven, and God's will is done in earth as it is in heaven.

You are the someone of God's kingdom. You have access to God's furnace. Your prayers move God to change the world. You may not understand the mystery of prayer. You don't need to. But this much is clear: Actions in heaven begin when someone prays on earth. What an amazing thought!

When you speak, Jesus hears.

And when Jesus hears, thunder falls.

And when thunder falls, the world is changed.

All because someone prayed.

CHAPTER 9

THE KITCHEN

Give us this day our daily bread . . .

I did a bit of research on the culture of the kitchen this week. Here is what I learned: people love to talk about food. If you're ever in need of a conversation prompter, try this one: "Do you know any curious dining practices?" There'll be no shortage of stories. The kitchen seems to be one place where all of us have some experience. In fact, you might say that some people are (ahem) heavyweights in this area. Ask people to relate curious eating habits and they'll give you a mouthful.

Like the uncle who pours syrup on everything he eats. ("Everything?" I asked the same question. *Everything*, I was assured.)

Like the father who puts gravy on his cake and the other father who eats his pie crust first. (Says he likes to save the point till last.)

Like the dad (mine) who crumbled his cornbread in buttermilk.

One remembered a verse:

> *I eat my peas with honey.*
> *I've done it all my life.*

It makes them taste funny.
But it keeps them on my knife.[1]

Another remembered an old wives' tale about eating ice cream with the spoon upside down to prevent headaches. More than one person was taught to eat bread after fish and never to drink milk with fish.

I was surprised how many hate to intermingle their servings. "First, I eat all my beans. Then all my corn. Then all my meat." (Correct me if I'm wrong, but aren't they about to be mixed anyway?) One fellow carries this to an extreme. Whereas many segregate their foods so they don't touch while on the plate, he puts each portion on its own saucer.

A history buff reminded me that kitchens in colonial America had a trough in the floor into which the bones would be tossed and near which the dogs would wait. Speaking of dogs, more than one person remembered the childhood days of smuggling unwanted food to their pet and then smiling innocently as mom applauded the clean plate.

Burps are welcome in China. And an empty plate among some Latin cultures only assures your host that you're still hungry. The practice of intersecting the fork and knife on a finished plate was begun by Italian nobility who saw the cross as an act of thanksgiving.[2]

Emily Post would have groaned at some of the earliest writings on etiquette. One written in the 1530s states: "If you can't swallow a piece of food, turn around discreetly and throw it somewhere."[3]

My favorite table morsel was the story of the man with nine sons. The rule of his kitchen was simple: Dad gets the last piece of chicken. If he doesn't want it, the fastest fork wins. One night, as all ten eyed the final piece on the plate, a thunderstorm caused an electrical blackout. There was a scream in the dark, and when the lights returned, the dad's hand was on the chicken platter with nine forks sticking in it.

Everybody has a kitchen story because everybody has a history in the kitchen. Whether yours was a campfire in the jungle or a culinary castle in Manhattan, you learned early that in this room your basic needs were supplied. A garage is optional. A living room is negotiable. An office is a luxury. But a kitchen? Absolutely essential. Every house has one. Even the Great House of God.

KITCHEN RULES

Or perhaps we should say *especially* the Great House of God. For who is more concerned with your basic needs than your Father in heaven? God is not a mountain guru only involved in the mystical and spiritual. The same hand that guides your soul gives food for your body. The One who clothes you in goodness is the same One who clothes you in cloth. In the school of life, God is both the teacher and the cook. He provides fire for the heart and food for the stomach. Your eternal salvation and your evening meal come from the same hand. There is a kitchen in God's Great House; let's journey downstairs and enjoy its warmth.

The table is long. The chairs are many and the food ample. On the wall hangs a simple prayer: *Give us this day our daily bread.* The words, though they be brief, raise some good questions. For example, where is the *please?* Dare we saunter into the presence of God and say, "Give us"? Another question concerns the paucity of the prayer. Just bread? Any chance for some spaghetti? And what about tomorrow? Why are we to pray for today's provisions and not those of the future?

Perhaps the best way to answer these questions is to look again at the wall of the kitchen. Beneath the prayer, *Give us this day our daily bread,* I can envision two statements. You might call them rules of the kitchen. You've seen such rules before. "No singing at the table." "Wash before you eat." "Carry your plate to the sink." "Max gets double portions of dessert." (I wish!)

God's kitchen has a couple of rules as well. The first is a rule of dependence:

RULE #1: DON'T BE SHY, ASK

The first word in the phrase, "Give us this day our daily bread," seems abrupt. Sounds terse, doesn't it? Too demanding. Wouldn't an "If you don't mind" be more appropriate? Perhaps a "Pardon me, but could I ask you to give . . ." would be better? Am I not being irreverent if I simply say, "Give us this day our daily bread"? Well, you are if this is where you begin. But it isn't. If you have followed Christ's model for prayer, your preoccupation has been his wonder rather than your stomach. The first three petitions are God-centered, not self-centered. Hallowed be your name . . . your kingdom come . . . your will be done.

Your first step into the house of God was not to the kitchen but to the living room, where you were reminded of your adoption. "Our *Father* who is in heaven." You then studied the foundation of the house, where you pondered his permanence. "Our Father *who is* in heaven." Next you entered the observatory and marveled at his handiwork: "Our Father who is in *heaven*." In the chapel, you worshiped his holiness: "Hallowed be thy name." In the throne room, you touched the lowered scepter and prayed the greatest prayer, "Thy kingdom come." In the study, you submitted your desires to his and prayed, "Thy will be done." And all of heaven was silent as you placed your prayer in the furnace, saying, "in earth as it is in heaven."

Proper prayer follows such a path, revealing God to us before revealing our needs to God. (You might reread that one.) The purpose of prayer is not to change God but to change us, and by the time we reach God's kitchen, we are changed people. Wasn't our heart warmed when we called him Father? Weren't our fears stilled when we contemplated his constancy? Weren't we amazed as we stared at the heavens?

Seeing his holiness caused us to confess our sin. Inviting his kingdom to come reminded us to stop building our own. Asking God for his will to be done placed our will in second place to his. And realizing that heaven pauses when we pray left us breathless in his presence.

By the time we step into the kitchen, we're renewed people! We've been comforted by our Father, conformed by his nature, consumed by our Creator, convicted by his character, constrained by his power, commissioned by our Teacher, and compelled by his attention to our prayers.

The prayer's next three petitions encompass all of the concerns of our life. *Our daily bread* addresses the present. *Forgive our sins* addresses the past. *Lead us not into temptation* speaks to the future. (The wonder of God's wisdom: how he can reduce all our needs to three simple statements.)

First he addresses our need for bread. The term means all of a person's physical needs. Martin Luther defined bread as "Everything necessary for the preservation of this life, including food, a healthy body, house, home, wife and children." This verse urges us to talk to God about the necessities of life. He may also give us the luxuries of life, but he certainly will grant the necessities.

Any fear that God wouldn't meet our needs was left in the observatory. Would he give the stars their glitter and not give us our food? Of course not. He has committed to care for us. We aren't wrestling crumbs out of a reluctant hand but, rather, confessing the bounty of a generous hand. The essence of the prayer is really an affirmation of the Father's care. Our provision is his priority.

Turn your attention to Psalm 37.

> Trust the Lord and do good. Live in the land and feed on truth. Enjoy serving the LORD, and he will give you what you want. Depend on the LORD; trust him, and he will take care of you. (vv. 3–5)

God is committed to caring for our needs. Paul wrote that a man who won't feed his own family is worse than an unbeliever (1 Tim. 5:8).

How much more will a holy God care for his children? After all, how can we fulfill his mission unless our needs are met? How can we teach or minister or influence unless we have our basic needs satisfied? Will God enlist us in his army and not provide a commissary? Of course not.

"I pray that the God of peace will give you every good thing you need so you can do what he wants" (Heb. 13:20). Hasn't that prayer been answered in our life? We may not have had a feast, but haven't we always had food? Perhaps there was no banquet, but at least there was bread. And many times there was a banquet.

In fact, many of us in the United States have trouble relating to the phrase "Give us this day our daily bread" because our pantries are so packed and our bellies so full we seldom ask for food. We ask for self-control. We don't say, "God, let me eat." We say, "God, help me not to eat so much." You won't find books in our stores on surviving starvation, but you'll find shelves loaded with books on losing weight. This doesn't negate the importance of this phrase, however. Just the opposite. For us, the blessed of belly, this prayer has double meaning.

We pray, only to find our prayer already answered! We are like the high school senior who decides to go to college and then learns the cost of tuition. He runs to his father and pleads, "I'm sorry to ask so much, Dad, but I have nowhere else to go. I want to go to college, and I don't have a penny." The father puts his arms around the son and smiles and says, "Don't worry, son. The day you were born I began saving for your education. I've already provided for your tuition."

The boy made the request only to find the father had already met it. The same happens to you. At some point in your life it occurs to you that someone is providing for your needs. You take a giant step in maturity when you agree with David's words in 1 Chronicles 29:14: "Everything we have has come from you, and we only give you what is yours already" (TLB). You may be writing a check and stirring the soup, but there's more to putting food on the table than that. What about the ancient symbiosis of the seed and the soil and the sun and the rain? Who created animals for food and minerals for metal? Long before you knew you needed someone to provide for your needs, God already had.

So the first rule in the kitchen is one of dependence. Ask God for whatever you need. He is committed to you. God lives with the self-assigned task of providing for his own, and so far, you've got to admit, he's done pretty well at the job.

The second rule is one of trust.

RULE #2: TRUST THE COOK

My informal survey on eating habits reminded me of the time I pigged out on a Pillsbury Dough tube. When I was a youngster, my mom would let me lick the bowl after she used it to stir the cookie dough. I remember thinking how great it would be to make a meal out of the gooey stuff. In college my dream came true.

Four of us friends went to a weekend retreat at a farm. On the way we stopped at a grocery store. As you can imagine, we were careful to select proper vegetables, skim milk, no-fat yogurt—and we stayed away from the sweets. We also drove by the White House and picked up the President and the First Lady to do our laundry. Are you kidding? We filled our basket with nothing but fantasy. And for me, my fantasy was cookie dough! This was going to be a Pillsbury Doughboy weekend. That night I peeled the plastic off the dough like the peeling off a banana and took a big bite . . . then another . . . then anothuuuther . . . then uhhh-nuuuther. Then . . . yuck. I'd had enough.

That usually happens when we make our own menu. You'll notice this is the first time we've used the word *menu*. The kitchen in God's house is no restaurant. It is not owned by a stranger, it is run by your

Father. It's not a place you visit and leave; it's a place to linger and chat. It's not open one hour and closed the next; the kitchen is ever available. You don't eat and then pay; you eat and say thanks. But perhaps the most important difference between a kitchen and a restaurant is the menu. A kitchen doesn't have one.

God's kitchen doesn't need one. Things may be different in your house, but in the house of God, the One who provides the food is the One who prepares the meal. We don't swagger into his presence and demand delicacies. Nor do we sit outside the door and hope for crumbs. We simply take our places at the table and gladly trust him to "Give us this day our daily bread."

What a statement of trust! Whatever you want me to have is all I want. In his book *Victorious Praying*, Alan Redpath translates the phrase, "Give us this day bread suited to our need."[4] Some days the plate runs over. God keeps bringing out more food, and we keep loosening our belt. A promotion. A privilege. A friendship. A gift. A lifetime of grace. An eternity of joy. There are times when we literally push ourselves back from the table, amazed at God's kindness. "You serve me a six-course dinner right in front of my enemies. You revive my drooping head; my cup brims with blessing" (Ps. 23:5 MSG).

And then there are those days when, well, when we have to eat our broccoli. Our daily bread could be tears or sorrow or discipline. Our portion may include adversity as well as opportunity.

This verse was on my mind last night during family devotions. I called my daughters to the table and set a plate in front of each. In the center of the table I placed a collection of food: some fruit, some raw vegetables, and some Oreo cookies. "Every day," I explained, "God prepares for us a plate of experiences. What kind of plate do you most enjoy?"

The answer was easy. Sara put three cookies on her plate. Some days are like that, aren't they? Some days are "three cookie days."

Many are not. Sometimes our plate has nothing but vegetables—twenty-four hours of celery, carrots, and squash. Apparently God knows we need some strength, and though the portion may be hard to swallow, isn't it for our own good? Most days, however, have a bit of it all. Vegetables, which are healthy but dull. Fruit, which tastes better, and we enjoy. And even an Oreo, which does little for our nutrition but a lot for our attitude.

All are important, and all are from God. "We know that in everything God works for the good of those who love him" (Rom. 8:28). We, like Paul, must learn the "secret of being happy at any time in everything that happens, when I have enough to eat and when I go hungry, when I have more than I need and when I do not have enough. I can do all things through Christ, because he gives me strength" (Phil. 4:12–13).

Perhaps the heart of the prayer is found in the book of Proverbs.

Give me enough food to live on, neither too much nor too little.
If I'm too full, I might get independent, saying, "God? Who needs him?" If I'm poor, I might steal and dishonor the name of my God.
(Prov. 30:8–9 MSG)

The next time your plate has more broccoli than apple pie, remember who prepared the meal. And the next time your plate has a portion you find hard to swallow, talk to God about it. Jesus did. In the garden of Gethsemane his Father handed him a cup of suffering so sour, so vile, that Jesus handed it back to heaven. "My Father," he prayed, "if it is possible, may this cup be taken from me. Yet not as I will, but as you will" (Matt. 26:39 NIV).

Even Jesus was given a portion he found hard to swallow. But with God's help, he did. And with God's help, you can too.

CHAPTER 10

THE ROOF

Forgive us our debts . . .

F orgive me for broaching the issue, but I must.

I realize the topic is personal, but it's time we went public.

I need to talk to you about being overdrawn at the bank. Your paycheck was late. Your landlord cashed your rent check too quickly. You were going to make a deposit, but your aunt called from Minnesota, and by the time you got to the bank, it was closed, and you didn't know how to make a night deposit.

Regardless of the reason, the result is the same: *insufficient funds.* What an ominous phrase. In the great gallery of famous phrases, "insufficient funds" hangs in the same hallway with "The IRS will audit your account," "A root canal is necessary," and "Let's stop dating and just be friends." Insufficient funds. (To get the full impact of the phrase, imagine hearing the words spoken by a man with fangs, black cape, and a deep voice in a Transylvanian castle. "You have insufficient funds.")

You are overdrawn. You gave more than you had to give. You spent more than you had to spend. And guess who has to cough up some cash? Not the bank; they didn't write the check. Not the store; they didn't make the purchase. Not your aunt in Minnesota, unless she's got a soft spot in her heart for you. In the grand scheme of things, you can make all the excuses we want, but a bounced check lands in the lap of the one who wrote it.

What do you do if you don't have any money? What do you do if you have nothing to deposit but an honest apology and good intentions? You pray that some wealthy soul will make a huge deposit in your account. If you're talking about your financial debt, that's not likely to happen. If you're talking about your spiritual debt, however, it already has.

Your Father has covered your shortfall. In God's house you are covered by the roof of his grace.

THE ROOF OF PROTECTION

The roof of a house is seldom noticed. How often do your guests enter your doorway saying, "You have one of the finest roofs I've ever seen!" We've had hundreds of people in and out of our home through the years, and I honestly can't remember one comment about the roof. They might remind me to cut the grass or clean my sidewalk, but compliment my roof? Not yet.

Such disregard is no fault of the builder. He and his crew labored hours, balancing beams and nailing shingles. Yet, in spite of their effort, most people would notice a two-dollar lamp before they would notice the roof.

Let's not make the same mistake. As God covered his Great House, he spared no expense. In fact, his roof was the most costly section of the structure. It cost him the life of his Son. He invites us to study his work by virtue of three words in the center of the prayer. "Forgive our debts."

WE OWE A DEBT WE CANNOT PAY

Debt. The Greek word for *debt* has no mystery. It simply means "to owe someone something." If to be in debt is to owe someone something, isn't it appropriate for us speak of debt in our prayer, for aren't we all in debt to God?

Aren't we in God's debt when we disobey his commands? He tells us to go south and we go north. He tells us to turn right and we turn left. Rather than love our neighbor, we hurt our neighbor. Instead of seeking his will, we seek our will. We're told to forgive our enemies, but we attack our enemies. We disobey God.

Aren't we in God's debt when we disregard him? He makes the universe and we applaud science. He heals the sick and we applaud medicine. He grants beauty and we credit Mother Nature. He gives us possessions and we salute human ingenuity.

Don't we go into debt when we disrespect God's children? What if I did to you what we do to God? What if I shouted at your child in your presence? What if I called him names or struck him? You wouldn't tolerate it. But don't we do the same? How does God feel when we mistreat one of his children? When we curse at his offspring? When we criticize a coworker, or gossip about a relative, or speak about someone before we speak to them? Aren't we in God's debt when we mistreat a neighbor?

"Wait a second, Max. You mean every time I do one of these things, I'm writing a check on my heavenly bank account?"

That's exactly what I'm saying. I'm also saying that if Christ had not covered us with his grace, each of us would be overdrawn on that account. When it comes to goodness we would have insufficient funds. Inadequate holiness. God requires a certain balance of virtue in our account, and it's more than any of us has alone. Our holiness account shows insufficient funds, and only the holy will see the Lord; what can we do?

We could try making a few deposits. Maybe if I wave at my neighbor or compliment my husband or go to church next Sunday, I'll get caught up. But how do you know when you've made enough? How many trips do I need to make to the bank? How much credit do I need? When can I relax?

That's the problem. You never can. "People cannot do any work that will make them right with God" (Rom. 4:5). If you are trying to justify your own statement, forget ever having peace. You're going to spend the rest of your days huffing and puffing to get to the drive-through window before the bank closes. You are trying to justify an account you can't justify. May I remind you of the roof of grace that covers you?

"It is God who justifies" (8:33 NIV).

GOD PAID A DEBT HE DID NOT OWE

God assigned himself the task of balancing your account. You cannot deal with your own sins. "Only God can forgive sins" (Mark 2:7). Jesus is "the Lamb of God, who takes away the sin of the world!" (John 1:29). It's not you.

How did God deal with your debt?

Did he overlook it? He could have. He could have burned the statement. He could have ignored your bounced checks. But would a holy God do that? *Could* a holy God do that? No. Else he wouldn't be holy. Besides, is that how we want God to run his world—ignoring our sin and thereby endorsing our rebellion?

Did he punish you for your sins? Again, he could have. He could have crossed your name out of the book and wiped you off the face of the earth. But would a loving God do that? *Could* a loving God do that? He loves you with an everlasting love. Nothing can separate you from his love.

So what did he do? "God put the world square with himself

through the Messiah, giving the world a fresh start by offering forgiveness of sins. . . . How? you ask. In Christ. God put the wrong on him who never did anything wrong, so we could be put right with God" (2 Cor. 5:19–21 MSG).

Don't miss what happened. He took your statement flowing with red ink and bad checks and put his name at the top. He took his statement, which listed a million deposits and not one withdrawal, and put your name at the top. He assumed your debt. You assumed his fortune. And that's not all he did.

He also paid your penalty. If you are overdrawn at a bank, a fine must be paid. If you are overdrawn with God, a penalty must be paid as well. The fine at the bank is a hassle. But the penalty from God is hell. Jesus not only balanced your account; he paid your penalty. He took your place and paid the price for your sins. "He changed places with us and put himself under that curse" (Gal. 3:13).

> That's what Christ did definitively: suffered because of others' sins, the Righteous One for the unrighteous ones. He went through it all—was put to death and then made alive—to bring us to God. (1 Pet. 3:18 MSG)

> But he was wounded for the wrong we did; he was crushed for the evil we did. The punishment, which made us well, was given to him, and we are healed because of his wounds. (Isa. 53:5)

"With one sacrifice [Jesus] made perfect forever those who are being made holy" (Heb. 10:14). No more sacrifice needs to be made. No more deposits are necessary. So complete was the payment that Jesus used a banking term to proclaim your salvation. "It is finished!" (John 19:30 NKJV). *Tetelestai* was a financial term used to announce the final installment, the ultimate payment.

Now, if the task is finished, is anything else required of you? Of course not. If the account is full, what more could you add? Even saying the phrase "forgive our debts" does not earn grace. We repeat the words to remind us of the forgiveness we have, not to attain a forgiveness we need. I'll say more about that in the next chapter, but before moving on, may we talk frankly?

For some of you these thoughts about bounced checks and God's grace aren't new, but aren't they precious? Honestly, have you ever been given a gift that compares to God's grace? Finding this treasure of mercy makes the poorest beggar a prince. Missing this gift makes the wealthiest man a pauper.

Again, many of you knew that. I pray the reminder encourages you.

But for others, this is more than good news . . . it is *new* news. You never knew there was a roof of grace. And what a grand roof it is. The tiles are thick, and the beams are sturdy. Under it you are shielded from the storms of guilt and shame. Beneath the covering of Christ, no accuser can touch you, and no act can condemn you.

Isn't it good to know you don't have to stand outside in the storm anymore?

"But is it big enough for me?" you ask. Well, it was big enough for one who denied Christ (Peter). One who mocked Christ (the thief on the cross). One who persecuted Christ (Paul). Yes, it's big enough for you. Though you've spent a lifetime writing insufficient checks, God has stamped these words on your statement: *my grace is sufficient for you.*

Picture, if you will, a blank check. The amount of the check is "sufficient grace." The signer of the check is Jesus. The only blank line is for the payee. That part is for you. May I urge you to spend a few moments with your Savior receiving this check? Reflect on the work of his grace. Look toward the roof. Its beams are from Calvary, and the nails once held a Savior to the cross. His sacrifice was for you.

Express your thanks for his grace. Whether for the first time or the thousandth, let him hear you whisper, "Forgive us our debts." And let him answer your prayer as you imagine writing your name on the check.

Perhaps I best slip out now and leave the two of you to talk. I'll be waiting in the hallway of the Great House of God.

CHAPTER 11

THE HALLWAY

GRACE RECEIVED, GRACE GIVEN

Forgive us our debts, as we also have forgiven our debtors. . . .
For if you forgive men when they sin against you, your
heavenly Father will also forgive you. But if you do not forgive
men their sins, your Father will not forgive your sins.

I'd like to talk to you about bounty hunters, nitro around the neck, one of the greatest principles in the Bible, and okra and anchovy sandwiches. But before I do, let's start with a thought about hit men.

Living in the crosshairs of a hit man is no treat. I should know. I had one after me for three months. He wasn't a Mafia member, nor was he a gang member. He didn't carry a gun with a scope; his weapons were even deadlier. He had a phone number and a commission—track me down and make me pay.

His job? Collect past-due payments for a credit card company.

I hope you'll believe me when I say I had paid my bill. He certainly didn't believe me. I knew I'd paid the bill—I had the canceled check to prove it. The only problem was that the check was on a boat with all our other belongings somewhere between Miami and Rio. We had just moved to Brazil, and our possessions were in transit. I wouldn't have access to my bank statement for three months. He wasn't about to wait that long.

He threatened to ruin my credit, sue the travel agency, and call the police; he even said he would tell my mother (the big tattletale). After weeks of calling me collect, he suddenly quit bugging me. No explanation. All I can figure is that he traced the error to north of the equator rather than south, and he left me alone. He also left me amazed. I remember asking Denalyn, "What kind of person would enjoy such a job? His profession is aggravation."

A good day for him means a bad day for everyone he contacts. Don't get me wrong. I understand why such an occupation is necessary. I just wonder, what kind of person would want such a job? Who wants to be a missionary of misery? Collectors spend the day making people feel bad. No one wants to take their calls. No one is happy to see them at the door. No one wants to read their letters. Can you imagine what their spouses say as they go to work? "Make 'em squirm, honey." Do their bosses motivate them with the "blood out of a turnip" award? Who is their hero? Godzilla? What a job. Their payday is in your paycheck, and they are out to get it. Can you imagine spending your days like that?

Perhaps you can. Perhaps all of us can. Even the best among us spend time demanding payment. Doesn't someone owe you something? An apology? A second chance? A fresh start? An explanation? A thank-you? A childhood? A marriage? Stop and think about it (which I don't encourage you to do for long), and you can make a list of a lot of folks who are in your debt. Your parents should have been more protective. Your children should have been more appreciative. Your spouse should be more sensitive. Your preacher should have been more attentive.

What are you going to do with those in your debt? People in your past have dipped their hands in your purse and taken what was yours. What are you going to do? Few questions are more important. Dealing with debt is at the heart of your happiness. It's also at the heart of the Lord's Prayer.

Having reminded us of the grace we have received, Jesus then spoke of the grace we should share.

> "Forgive us our debts, as we also have forgiven our debtors. . . . For if
> you forgive men when they sin against you, your heavenly Father will
> also forgive you. But if you do not forgive men their sins, your Father
> will not forgive your sins." (Matt. 6:12–15 NIV)

Through the center of the Great House of God runs a large hallway. You can't get from one room to another without using it. Want to leave the kitchen and go to the study? Use the corridor. Want to take the stairs to the chapel? Use the corridor. You can't go anywhere without walking the hallway. And you can't walk the hallway without bumping into people.

Jesus does not question the reality of your wounds. He does not doubt that you have been sinned against. The issue is not the existence of pain; the issue is the treatment of pain. What are you going to do with your debts?

Dale Carnegie tells about a visit to Yellowstone Park, where he saw a grizzly bear. The huge animal was in the center of a clearing, feeding on some discarded camp food. For several minutes he feasted alone; no other creature dared draw near. After a few moments a skunk walked through the meadow toward the food and took his place next to the grizzly. The bear didn't object, and Carnegie knew why. "The grizzly," he said, "knew the high cost of getting even."[1]

We'd be wise to learn the same. Settling the score is done at great expense.

THE HIGH COST OF GETTING EVEN

For one thing, you pay a price relationally.

Have you ever noticed in the Western movies how the bounty hunter travels alone? It's not hard to see why. Who wants to hang out with a guy who settles scores for a living? Who wants to risk getting on his bad side? More than once I've heard a person spew his anger. He thought I was listening, when really I was thinking, *I hope I never get on his list.* Cantankerous sorts, these bounty hunters. Best leave them alone. Hang out with the angry, and you might catch a stray bullet. Debt-settling is a lonely occupation. It's also an unhealthy occupation.

You pay a high price physically.

The Bible says it best. "Resentment kills a fool" (Job 5:2 NIV). It reminds me of an old Amos and Andy routine. Amos asks Andy what that little bottle is he's wearing around his neck. "Nitroglycerine," he answers. Amos is stunned that Andy would be wearing a necklace of nitro, so he asks for an explanation. Andy tells him about a fellow who has a bad habit of poking people in the chest while he's speaking. "It drives me crazy," Andy says. "I'm wearing this nitro so the next time he pokes me, I'll blow his finger off."

Andy's not the first to forget that when you try to get even, you get hurt. Job was right when he said, "You tear yourself to pieces in your anger" (Job 18:4). Ever notice that we describe the people who bug us as a "pain in the neck"? Whose neck are we referring to? Certainly not theirs. We are the ones who suffer.

Some time ago I was speaking about anger at a men's gathering. I described resentment as a prison and pointed out that when we put someone in our jail cell of hatred, we are stuck guarding the door. After the message a man introduced himself as a former prison inmate. He described how the guard at the gate of a prison is even more confined than a prisoner. The guard spends his day in a four-by-five-foot house.

The prisoner has a ten-by-twelve-foot cell. The guard can't leave, the prisoner gets to walk around. The prisoner can relax, but the guard has to be constantly alert. You might object and say, "Yes, but the guard of the prison gets to go home at night." True, but the guard of the prison of resentment doesn't.

If you're out to settle the score, you'll never rest. How can you? For one thing, your enemy may never pay up. As much as you think you deserve an apology, your debtor may not agree. The racist may never repent. The chauvinist may never change. As justified as you are in your quest for vengeance, you may never get a penny's worth of justice. And if you do, will it be enough?

Let's really think about this one. How much justice is enough? Picture your enemy for a moment. Picture him tied to the whipping post. The strong-armed man with the whip turns to you and asks, "How many lashes?" And you give a number. The whip cracks and the blood flows and the punishment is inflicted. Your foe slumps to the ground and you walk away.

Are you happy now? Do you feel better? Are you at peace? Perhaps for a while, but soon another memory will surface and another lash will be needed and . . . when does it all stop?

It stops when you take seriously the words of Jesus. Read them again: "Forgive us our debts, as we also have forgiven our debtors. . . . For if you forgive men when they sin against you, your heavenly Father will also forgive you. But if you do not forgive men their sins, your Father will not forgive your sins."

Through this verse we learn the greatest cost of getting even. I've suggested that you pay a high price relationally and physically, but Jesus has a far more important reason for you to forgive. If you don't, you pay a high price spiritually.

Before we discuss what these verses mean, it would be wise to point out what they do not mean. The text does not suggest that we earn

God's grace by giving grace. At first blush, the phrase appears to present a type of triangular peace treaty. "If I forgive my enemy, then God will forgive me." A casual reading suggests we earn our forgiveness by offering forgiveness to others. Mercy is a merit that saves me. Such an interpretation is impossible for the simple reason that it conflicts with the rest of Scripture. If we can attain forgiveness by forgiving others (or any other good work), then why do we need a Savior? If we can pay for our sins through our mercy, why did Jesus die for our sins? If salvation is a result of our effort, then why did Paul insist, "You have been saved by grace through believing. You did not save yourselves; it was a gift from God" (Eph. 2:8).

Salvation is a free gift.

The question from the last chapter surfaces again. If we are already forgiven, then why does Jesus teach us to pray, "Forgive us our debts"?

The very reason you would want your children to do the same. If my children violate one of my standards or disobey a rule, I don't disown them. I don't kick them out of the house or tell them to change their last name. But I do expect them to be honest and apologize. And until they do, the tenderness of our relationship will suffer. The nature of the relationship won't be altered, but the intimacy will.

The same happens in our walk with God. Confession does not create a relationship with God, it simply nourishes it. If you are a believer, admission of sins does not alter your position before God, but it does enhance your peace with God. When you confess, you agree; you quit arguing with God and agree with him about your sin. Unconfessed sin leads to a state of disagreement. You may be God's child, but you don't want to talk to him. He still loves you, but until you admit what you've done, there's going to be tension in the house.

But just as unconfessed sin hinders joy, confessed sin releases it.

When we admit sin we are like a first grader standing before the teacher with a messy paper. "I colored outside the lines too many times. Could I start over on a clean sheet?" "Of course," says the teacher. Happy is the first grader who gets a second chance or, as David wrote, "Happy is the person whose sins are forgiven, whose wrongs are pardoned" (Ps. 32:1). So we dash back to our seat and start over.

Would there ever be a case when the teacher would leave you to draw on your soiled paper? There might be. I can think of one example when the teacher might refuse to give you a second chance. Suppose she witnesses your mistreatment of the kid in the next desk. A few minutes earlier she saw him ask you for a piece of paper out of your tablet, and you refused. Though you had plenty to give, you clutched your Big Chief with both hands and refused to share. And now here you are making the same request of her?

Who would blame her if she said, "I tell you what, I'm going to grant you the same kindness you gave your classmate. The way you treat Harry is the way I'll treat you. You're still my student, and I'm still your teacher. I'm not kicking you out of class, but I am going to give you a chance to learn a lesson." Now we're getting down to the nitty-gritty of the verse, for this is exactly what the phrase means: Forgive us our debts as we have forgiven our debtors.

One of the Greatest Principles in the Bible

"Treat me as I treat my neighbor." Are you aware that this is what you are saying to your Father? Give me what I give them. Grant me the same peace I grant others. Let me enjoy the same tolerance I offer. God will treat you the way you treat others.

In any given Christian community there are two groups: those who are contagious in their joy and those who are cranky in their faith. They've accepted Christ and are seeking him, but their balloon has no helium. One is grateful, the other is grumpy. Both are saved. Both are heaven bound. But one sees the rainbow and the other sees the rain.

Could this principle explain the difference? Could it be that they are experiencing the same joy they have given their offenders? One says, "I forgive you," and feels forgiven. The other says, "I'm ticked off," and lives ticked off at the world.

Elsewhere Jesus said:

"Don't judge others, and you will not be judged. Don't accuse others of being guilty, and you will not be accused of being guilty. *Forgive, and you will be forgiven. Give, and you will receive.* You will be given much. Pressed down, shaken together, and running over, it will spill into your lap. The way you give to others is the way God will give to you." (Luke 6:37–38, emphasis mine)

It's as if God sends you to the market to purchase your neighbor's groceries saying, "Whatever you get your neighbor, get also for yourself. For whatever you give him is what you receive."

Pretty simple system. I'm not too bright, but I can figure this one out. I love thick, juicy hamburger meat, so I buy my neighbor thick, juicy hamburger meat. I'm crazy about double-chocolate ice cream, so I buy my neighbor double-chocolate ice cream. And when I drink milk, I don't want the skimpy skim stuff that Denalyn makes me drink. I want Christian milk, just like God made it. So what do I buy my neighbor? Christian milk, just like God made it.

Let's take this a step further. Suppose your neighbor's trash blows into your yard. You mention the mess to him, and he says he'll get to it sometime next week. You inform him that you've got company coming and couldn't he get out of that chair and do some work? He tells you not to be so picky, that the garbage fertilizes your garden. You're just about to walk across the lawn to have a talk when God reminds you, "Time to go to the market and buy your neighbor's groceries." So you grumble and mumble your way to the store, and then it hits you, "I'll get even with the old bum." You go straight to the skim milk. Then you make a beeline to the anchovies and sardines. You march right past the double-chocolate ice cream and head toward the okra and rice. You make a final stop in the day-old bread section and pick up a crusty loaf with green spots on the edge.

Chuckling, you drive back to the house and drop the sack in the lap of your lazy, good-for-nothing neighbor. "Have a good dinner." And you walk away.

All your brilliant scheming left you hungry, so you go to your refrigerator to fix a sandwich, but guess what you find? Your pantry is full of what you gave your enemy. All you have to eat is exactly what you just bought. We get what we give.

Some of you have been eating sardines for a long time. Your diet ain't gonna change until you change. You look around at other Christians. They aren't as sour as you are. They're enjoying the delicacies of God, and you're stuck with okra and anchovies on moldy bread. You've always wondered why they look so happy and you feel so cranky. Maybe now you know. Could it be God is giving you exactly what you're giving someone else?

Would you like a change of menu? Earlier I referred to a men's conference where I spoke on the topic of anger. A couple of weeks after I returned home, I received this letter from a man named Harold Staub.

Max,

Thank you so much for speaking on forgiveness at Promise Keepers in Syracuse, NY, on June 7 and 8. I was there. Just want you to know I went home, talked to my wife on many subjects about forgiveness—the best two weeks of my life. You see, she went home to be with the Lord on June 24, totally forgiven. How wonderful is his love. Thank you so very much.[2]

When we called Harold to ask his permission to print his letter, he shared the touching details of his final days with his wife. He didn't know she was near death, nor did she. He did know, however, that some unresolved issues lay between them. Upon arriving home, he went to her, knelt before her, and asked forgiveness for anything he'd ever done. The gesture opened a floodgate of emotions, and the two talked late into the night. The initial effort at reconciliation continued for two weeks. The marriage enjoyed a depth not yet known. When Harold's wife died suddenly of an embolism, he was shocked. But he was ready, and now he is at peace.

What about you? Would you like some peace? Then quit giving your neighbor such a hassle. Want to enjoy God's generosity? Then let others enjoy yours. Would you like assurance that God forgives you? I think you know what you need to do.

So what will you be eating? Chocolate ice cream or okra? It's up to you.

CHAPTER 12

THE FAMILY ROOM

LEARNING TO LIVE TOGETHER

Our . . .

We are much like Ruth and Verena Cady. Since their birth in 1984 they have shared much. Just like any twins, they have shared a bike, a bed, a room, and toys. They've shared meals and stories and TV shows and birthdays. They shared the same womb before they were born and the same room after they were born. But the bond between Ruthie and Verena goes even further. They share more than toys and treats; they share the same heart.

Their bodies are fused together from the sternum to the waist. Though they have separate nervous systems and distinct personalities, they are sustained by the same, singular three-chambered heart. Neither could survive without the other. Since separation is not an option, cooperation becomes an obligation.

They have learned to work together. Take walking, for example. Their mother assumed they would take turns walking forward or backward. It made sense to her that they would alternate; one facing the front and the other the back. The girls had a better idea. They learned to walk sideways, almost like dancing. And they dance in the same direction.

They've learned to make up for each other's weaknesses. Verena loves to eat, but Ruthie finds sitting at the table too dull. Ruthie may eat only a half cup of fruit a day. No problem, her sister will eat enough for both. It's not unusual for her to have three bowls of cereal, two yogurts and two pieces of toast for breakfast. Ruthie tends to get restless while her sister eats and has been known to throw a bowl of ice cream across the room. This could lead to discipline for her but also has consequences for her sister.[1]

When one has to sit in the corner, so does the other. The innocent party doesn't complain; both learned early that they are stuck together for the good and the bad. Which is just one of the many lessons these girls can teach those of us who live in God's Great House.

Don't we share the same kitchen? Aren't we covered by the same roof and protected by the same walls? We don't sleep in the same bed, but we sleep under the same sky. We aren't sharing one heart . . . but then again, maybe we are, for don't we share the same hope for eternity, the same hurt from rejection, and the same hunger to be loved? Like the Cady twins, don't we have the same Father?

We don't pray to *my* Father or ask for *my* daily bread or ask God to forgive *my* sins. In God's house we speak the language of plurality: *our* Father, *our* daily bread, *our* debts, *our* debtors, lead *us* not into temptation, and deliver *us*.

The abundance of plural pronouns escorts us into one of the most colorful rooms in the house, the family room.

THE FAMILY ROOM

If you'd like a reminder of our Father's creativity, you'll find one here. We all call God "Father" and we all call Christ "Savior," but beyond

unity- we are one
It is church, not churches

that, things are quite diverse. Take a walk around the room and see what I mean.

Shoot some snooker with the bikers at the pool table.

Pick up a Swahili phrase from the tribesmen.

Eavesdrop on the theologians discussing dispensationalism.

Experience worship with a bagpipe, then cross the room and try the same with the accordion.

Ask the missionary if she ever gets lonely and the Bible translator if he ever gets confused.

Hear the testimony of the murderer and the music of the minstrel.

And if you're wondering how those folks from the other denominations got here, ask them. (They may want to ask you the same question.) Oh, the diversity of God's family.

We are olive-skinned, curly-haired, blue-eyed, and black.
We come from boarding schools and ghettos, mansions and shacks.
We wear turbans, we wear robes. We like tamales. We eat rice.
We have convictions and opinions, and to agree would be nice,
but we don't, still we try and this much we know:
'Tis better inside with each other than outside living alone.

Quite a family, wouldn't you agree? From God's perspective we have much in common. Jesus lists these common denominators in his prayer. They are easy to find. Every time we see the word *our* or *us*, we find a need.

Are Children in Need of a Father?

During the writing of this book, my daughter Jenna and I spent several days in the old city of Jerusalem. (I've promised to take each of my daughters to Jerusalem when they're twelve years old. Got the idea from Joseph.) One afternoon, as we were exiting the Jaffa gate, we found ourselves behind an orthodox Jewish family—a father and his three small girls. One of the daughters, perhaps four or five years of age, fell a few steps behind and couldn't see her father. "*Abba!*" she called to him. He stopped and looked. Only then did he realize he was separated from his daughter. "*Abba!*" she called again. He spotted her and immediately extended his hand. She took it, and I took mental notes as they continued. I wanted to see the actions of an *abba*.

He held her hand tightly in his as they descended the ramp. When he stopped at a busy street, she stepped off the curb, so he pulled her back. When the signal changed, he led her and her sisters through the intersection. In the middle of the street, he reached down and swung her up into his arms and continued their journey.

Isn't that what we all need? An *abba* who will hear when we call? Who will take our hand when we're weak? Who will guide us through the hectic intersections of life? Don't we all need an *abba* who will swing us up into his arms and carry us home? We all need a father.

We Are Beggars in Need of Bread

Not only are we children in need of a father, we are also beggars in need of bread. "Give us this day our daily bread," we pray.

You may not appreciate my using the term *beggar*. You may prefer the word *hungry*. "We are all hungry, in need of bread." Such a phrase certainly has more dignity than the word *beggar*. Who wants to be called a beggar? Didn't you earn the money to buy the bread that sits on your table? Who are you to beg for anything? In fact, you may even find the word *hungry* offensive. To be hungry is to admit a basic need, something we sophisticated people are reluctant to do. Let me think, there must be a better phrase. How about this one? We aren't beggars, nor are we hungry; we are simply "abdominally challenged." There, that's better! "Abdominally challenged, in need of bread." You maintain a sense of independence with that word.

After all, you are ultimately responsible for the food you eat, right? Didn't you create the ground in which the seed was sown? No? Well, at least you made the seed? You didn't? What about the sun? Did you provide the heat during the day? Or the rain, did you send the clouds? No? Then exactly what did you do? You harvested food you didn't make from an earth you didn't create.

Let me see if I have this straight. Had God not done his part, you would have no food on your table. Hmmm, perhaps we best return to the word *beggar*. We are all beggars, in need of bread.

SINNERS IN NEED OF GRACE

We share one other need: We are sinners in need of grace, strugglers in need of strength. Jesus teaches us to pray, "Forgive us our debts . . . and lead us not into temptation."

We've all made mistakes, and we'll all make some more. The line that separates the best of us from the worst of us is a narrow one; hence we'd be wise to take seriously Paul's admonition:

Why do you judge your brothers or sisters in Christ? And why do you think you are better than they are? We will all stand before God to be judged, because it is written in the Scriptures: "As surely as I live, says the Lord, "everyone will bow before me; everyone will say that I am God." (Rom. 14:10–11)

Your sister would like me to remind you that she needs grace. Just like you need forgiveness, so does she. There comes a time in every relationship when it's damaging to seek justice, when settling the score only stirs the fire. There comes a time when the best thing you can do is accept your brother and offer him the same grace you've been given.

That's what Jenna did.

Earlier I mentioned our recent trip to Israel. I'll conclude by referring to it one more time. She and I boarded a 1:00 a.m. flight in Tel Aviv that would carry us back to the States. Traveling is always hectic, but that night it was especially bad. The plane was packed, and we were delayed because of extra-tight airport security. As we boarded, I realized that our seats weren't together. We were separated by an aisle. With no time to seek help from the front desk, I determined to persuade the fellow sitting next to Jenna to swap seats with me. *Surely he'll understand*, I thought. He didn't. He was already nestled down for the ten-hour flight and wasn't about to move. "Please," I begged, "let me sit by my daughter."

"I'm not moving."

"Come on, sir. Let's trade places."

He leaned up and looked at my seat and leaned back. "No thanks," he declined.

Growl. I took my seat, and Jenna took hers next to the thoughtless, heartless scoundrel. As the plane prepared for takeoff, I dedicated my mind to drawing a mental sketch of the jerk. Wasn't hard. Only a glance or two in his direction and I had him pegged as a terrorist on his way to assassinate the president of our country. By the time the plane was backing up, I was plotting how I'd trip him if he dared walk to the restroom during the flight. No doubt he'd smuggled a gun on board and it would fall to me to apprehend him.

I turned to intimidate him with a snarl and saw, much to my surprise, Jenna offering him a pretzel. What? My daughter fraternizing with the enemy! And even worse, he took it! As if the pretzel were an olive branch, he accepted her gift, and they both leaned their seats back and dozed off.

I eventually dozed myself but not before I'd learned the lesson God had used my daughter to teach me.

In God's house we occasionally find ourselves next to people we don't like. If we could ask them to leave, we would, but we aren't given the option. All of us are here by grace, and at some point, all of us have to share some grace. So the next time you find yourself next to a questionable character, don't give him a hard time . . . give him a pretzel.

CHAPTER 13

THE WALLS

SATAN, GOD'S SERVANT

And lead us not into temptation, but deliver us from the evil one . . .

The small population of people who saw me play school athletics have never questioned my decision to enter the ministry. I have, however, received a letter reminding me of the time I deep-snapped a football over the punter's head. Another former classmate reminisced with me about the fly ball that slipped out of my glove and allowed the winning run to score. And then there was the time my buddy scored a touchdown on an eighty-yard punt return only to have it called back because his buddy, yours truly, got penalized for clipping. Oh, the pain of such memories. They hurt, not just because I messed up but because I helped the other team. It's bad to lose; it's worse still to help your opponent win!

My most blatant experience of aiding the opposition occurred in a sixth-grade basketball tournament. I can't remember the exact score when I finally got to play, but I know it was close. I recall a loose ball, a scramble to grab it, and complete surprise when my teammate on the bottom of the pile threw it to me. When I saw that no one was between me and the basket, I took off. With the style of an MVP-to-be, I made a layup worthy of airtime on ESPN. My surprise at the ease of the basket was surpassed only by my surprise at the silence of the crowd.

No one applauded! Rather than pat me on the back, my team buried their faces in their hands. That's when I realized what I'd done. I'd made a basket on the wrong end of the court—I'd aided the enemy! I'd helped the wrong team. No wonder no one tried to stop me—I was helping their side.

Can you imagine how silly I felt?

If you can, then you can imagine how silly Satan must feel. Such is the pattern of the devil's day. Every time he sets out to score one for evil, he ends up scoring a point for good. When he schemes to thwart the kingdom, he always advances it. May I offer a few examples from the Bible?

BACKFIRES OF HELL

Remember Abraham's wife, Sarah? God promised her a child, but she remained childless for decades. Satan used an empty crib to stir up tension and dissension and doubt. Sarah would serve as his *prima facie* evidence as to why you can't trust God. In the end, she modeled just the opposite. The thought of this ninety-year-old in the maternity ward has instructed millions that God saves the best for last.

How about Moses? Satan and his horde howled with delight the day the young prince was run out of Egypt by the very people he wanted to deliver. They thought they'd derailed God's plan, when actually they'd played into God's hand. God used the defeat to humble his servant and the wilderness to train him. The result stood before Pharaoh forty years later, a seasoned Moses who'd learned to listen to God and survive in the desert.

And what about Daniel? The sight of Jerusalem's best young men being led into captivity appeared to be a victory for Satan. Hell's strategy was to isolate the godly young men. Again, the plan boomeranged. What Satan intended as captivity, God used for royalty. Daniel was soon asked to serve in the king's court. The very man Satan sought to silence spent most of his life praying to the God of Israel and advising the kings of Babylon.

And consider Paul. Satan hoped the prison would silence his pulpit, and it did, but it also unleashed his pen. The letters to the Galatians, Ephesians, Philippians, and Colossians were all written in a jail cell. Can't you just see Satan kicking the dirt and snarling his lips every time a person reads those epistles? He helped write them!

Peter is another example. Satan sought to discredit Jesus by provoking Peter to deny him. But the plan backfired. Rather than be an example of how far a fellow can fall, Peter became an example of how far God's grace extends.

Every time Satan scores a basket, the other team gets the points. He's the Colonel Klink of the Bible. For those of you who don't remember, Klink was the fall guy for Hogan on the television series *Hogan's Heroes.* (The sitcom ran from the mid-sixties to the early seventies.) Klink supposedly ran a German POW camp during World War II. Those inside the camp, however, knew better. They knew who *really* ran the camp: the prisoners. They listened to Klink's calls and read his mail. They even gave Klink ideas, all the while using him for their own cause.

Over and over the Bible makes it clear who really runs the earth. Satan may strut and prance, but it's God who calls the shots.

DELIVER US FROM THE EVIL ONE

The next-to-last phrase in the Lord's Prayer is a petition for protection from Satan: "And lead us not into temptation, but deliver us from the evil one" (Matt. 6:13 NIV).

Is such a prayer necessary? Would God ever lead us into temptation? James 1:13 says, "When people are tempted, they should not say, 'God is tempting me.' Evil cannot tempt God, and God himself does not tempt anyone." If God does not tempt us, then why pray, "Lead us not into temptation"? These words trouble the most sophisticated theologian.

But they don't trouble a child. And this is a prayer for the child-like heart. This is a prayer for those who look upon God as their *Abba*. This is a prayer for those who have already talked to their Father about provision for today ("Give us this day our daily bread.") and pardon for yesterday ("Forgive us our debts."). Now the child needs assurance about protection for tomorrow.

The phrase is best understood with a simple illustration. Imagine a father and son walking down an icy street. The father cautions the boy to be careful, but the boy is too excited to slow down. He hits the first patch of ice. Up go the feet and down plops the bottom. Dad comes along and helps him to his feet. The boy apologizes for disregarding the warning and then, tightly holding his father's big hand, he asks, "Keep me from the slippery spots. Don't let me fall again."

The Father is so willing to comply. "The steps of the godly are directed by the Lord. He delights in every detail of their lives. Though they stumble, they will not fall, for the Lord holds them by the hand" (Ps. 37:23–24 TLB). Such is the heart of this petition. It's a tender request of a child to a father. The last few slips have taught us—the walk is too treacherous to make alone. So we place our small hand in his large one and say, "Please, *Abba*, keep me from evil."

THE EVIL ONE

Besides, who else would we trust to deliver us from the Evil One? We have heard of this devil. And what we've heard disturbs us. Twice in Scripture the curtain of time is pulled back, and we are granted a glimpse at the most foolish gamble in history. Satan was an angel who was not content to be near God; he had to be above God. Lucifer was not satisfied to give God worship; he wanted to occupy God's throne.

According to Ezekiel, both Satan's beauty and evil were unequaled among the angels:

> "You were an example of what was perfect, full of wisdom and perfect in beauty. You had a wonderful life, as if you were in Eden, the garden of God. Every valuable gem was upon you. . . . You walked among the gems that shined like fire. Your life was right and good from the day you were created, until evil was found in you." (Ezek. 28:12–15)

The angels, like humans, were made to serve and worship God. The angels, like humans, were given free will. Otherwise, how could they worship? Both Isaiah and Ezekiel describe an angel more powerful than any human, more beautiful than any creature, yet more foolish than any being who has ever lived. His pride was his downfall.

Most scholars point to Isaiah 14:13–15 as the description of Lucifer's tumble:

> "I will go up to heaven. I will put my throne above God's stars. I will sit on the mountains of the gods, on the slopes of the sacred mountain. I will go up above the tops of the clouds. I will be like God Most High."

You can't miss the cadence of arrogance in the words: "I will . . . I will . . . I will . . . I will . . . I will." Because he sought to be like God, he fell away from God and has spent history trying to convince us to do the same. Isn't that the strategy he used with Eve? "You will be like God!" he promised (Gen. 3:5).

God uses Satan as part as His good plan.

He has not changed. He is as self-centered now as he was then. He is as foolish now as he was then. And he is just as limited now as he was then. Even when Lucifer's heart was good, he was inferior to God. All angels are inferior to God. God knows everything; they know only what he reveals. God is everywhere; they can be in only one place. God is all-powerful; angels are only as powerful as God allows them to be. All angels, including Satan, are inferior to God. And this may surprise you:

Satan is still a servant to God.

THE DEVIL IS "GOD'S DEVIL"

He doesn't want to be. He doesn't intend to be. He would like nothing more than to build his own kingdom, but he can't. Every time he tries to advance his cause, he ends up advancing God's.

Erwin Lutzer articulates this thought in his book, *The Serpent of Paradise:*

> The devil is just as much God's servant in his rebellion as he was in the days of his sweet obedience. . . . We can't quote Luther too often: The devil is God's devil.
>
> Satan has different roles to play, depending on God's counsel and purposes. He is pressed into service to do God's will in the world; he must do the bidding of the Almighty. We must bear in mind that he does have frightful powers, but knowing that those can only be exercised under God's direction and pleasure gives us hope. Satan is simply not free to wreak havoc on people at will.[1]

Satan doing the bidding of the Almighty? Seeking the permission of God? Does such language strike you as strange? It may. If it does, you can be sure Satan would rather you not hear what I'm about to say to you. He'd much rather you be deceived into thinking of him as an independent force with unlimited power. He doesn't want me to tell you about the walls that surround the Great House of God. Satan cannot climb them; he cannot penetrate them. He has absolutely no power, except that power that God permits.

He'd rather you never hear the words of John, "God's Spirit, who is in you, is greater than the devil, who is in the world" (1 John 4:4). And he'd certainly rather you never learn how God uses the devil as an instrument to advance the cause of Christ.

How does God use Satan to do the work of heaven? God uses Satan to:

1. *Refine the faithful.* We all have the devil's disease. Even the meekest among us have a tendency to think too highly of ourselves. Apparently Paul did. His résumé was impressive: a personal audience with Jesus, a participant in heavenly visions, an apostle chosen by God, an author of the Bible. He healed the sick, traveled the world, and penned some of history's greatest documents. Few could rival his achievements. And maybe he knew it. Perhaps there was a time when Paul began to pat himself on the back. God, who loved Paul and hates pride, protected Paul from the sin. And he used Satan to do it.

"To keep me from becoming conceited because of these surpassingly great revelations, there was given me a thorn in my flesh, a messenger of Satan, to torment me" (2 Cor. 12:7 NIV).

We aren't told the nature of the thorn, but we are told its purpose: to keep Paul humble. We are also told its origin—a messenger from Satan. The messenger could have been a pain, a problem, or a person who was a pain. We don't know. But we do know the messenger was under God's control. Please note verses 8 and 9, "Three times I pleaded with the Lord to take it away from me. But he said to me, 'My grace is sufficient for you, for my power is made perfect in weakness'" (NIV).

Satan and his forces were simply a tool in the hand of God to strengthen a servant.

Another example of the devil as God's servant is the temptation of Job. The devil dares to question the stability of Job's faith, and God gives him permission to test Job. "All right, then," God said. "Everything Job has is in your power, but you must not touch Job himself" (Job 1:12). Note that God set both the permission and parameters of the struggle. Job passes the test, and Satan complains, stating that Job would have fallen had he been forced to face pain. Again, God gives permission, and again, God gives the parameters. "Job is in your power," he told Satan, "but you may not take his life" (2:6).

Though the pain and the questions are abundant, in the end Job's faith and health are greater than ever. Again, we may not understand the reason for the test, but we know its source. Read this verse from the last chapter. The family of Job "comforted him and made him feel better about the trouble *the* Lord had brought on him" (42:11, emphasis mine).

Satan has no power except that which God gives him.

To the first-century church at Smyrna, Christ said, "Do not be afraid of what you are about to suffer. I tell you, the devil will put some of you in prison to test you, and you will suffer for ten days. But be faithful, even if you have to die, and I will give you the crown of life" (Rev. 2:10).

Analyze Jesus' words for a minute. Christ informed the church of the persecution, the duration of the persecution (ten days), the reason for the persecution (to test you), and the outcome of the persecution (a crown of life). In other words, Jesus used Satan to fortify his church.

Colonel Klink blows another one. Satan scores again for the other team. Don't you know that bugs him? Even when he appears to win, he loses. Martin Luther was right on target when he described the devil as God's tool, a hoe used to care for his garden. The hoe never cuts what the gardener intends to save and never saves what the gardener intends to weed. Surely a part of Satan's punishment is the frustration he feels in unwillingly serving as a tool to create a garden for God. Satan is used by God to refine the faithful.

God also uses the devil to:

2. *Awaken the sleeping.* Hundreds of years before Paul, another Jewish leader battled with his ego, but he lost. Saul, the first king of Israel, was consumed with jealousy. He was upstaged by David, the youngest son of a shepherding family. David did everything better than Saul: he sang better; he impressed the women more; he even killed the giants Saul feared. But rather than celebrate David's God-given abilities, Saul grew insanely hostile. God, in an apparent effort to awaken Saul from this fog of jealousy, enlisted the help of his unwilling servant, Satan. "The next day an evil spirit from God rushed upon Saul, and he prophesied in his house" (1 Sam. 18:10).

Observe a solemn principle: There are times when hearts grow so hard and ears so dull that God turns us over to endure the consequence of our choices. In this case, the demon was released to torment Saul. If Saul would not drink from the cup of God's kindness, let him spend some time drinking from the cup of hell's fury. "Let him be driven to despair that he might be driven back into the arms of God."[2]

The New Testament refers to incidents where similar discipline is administered. Paul chastises the church in Corinth for their tolerance of immorality. About an adulterer in the church he says:

> Then hand this man over to Satan. So his sinful self will be destroyed, and his spirit will be saved on the day of the Lord. (1 Cor. 5:5)

Paul gives comparable instruction to Timothy. The young evangelist was dealing with two disciples who'd made a shipwreck of their faith and had negatively influenced others. His instruction to Timothy?

"Hymenaeus and Alexander have done that, and I have given them to Satan so they will learn not to speak against God" (1 Tim. 1:20).

As drastic as it may appear, God will actually allow a person to experience hell on earth, in hopes of awakening his faith. A holy love makes the tough choice to release the child to the consequences of his rebellion.

By the way, doesn't this help explain the rampant evil that exists in the world? If God allows us to endure the consequences of our sin and the world is full of sinners, then the world is going to abound in evil. Isn't this what Paul meant in the first chapter of Romans? After describing those who worship the creation rather than the Creator, Paul said, "God left them and let them do the shameful things they wanted to do" (Rom. 1:26). Does God enjoy seeing the heartbreak and addictions of his children? No more than a parent enjoys disciplining a child. But holy love makes tough choices.

Remember, discipline should result in mercy, not misery. Some saints are awakened by a tap on the shoulder while others need a two-by-four to the head. And whenever God needs a two-by-four, Satan gets the call. He also gets the call to:

3. *Teach the church.* Perhaps the clearest illustration of how God uses Satan to achieve his purposes is found in the life of Peter. Listen to the warning Jesus gave to him: "Simon, Simon, Satan has asked to test all of you as a farmer sifts his wheat. I have prayed that you will not lose your faith! Help your brothers be stronger when you come back to me" (Luke 22:31–32).

Again notice who is in control. Even though Satan had a plan, he had to get permission. "All authority in heaven and on earth has been given to me" (Matt. 28:18 NIV), Jesus explained, and this is proof. The wolf cannot get to the sheep without permission of the Shepherd, and the Shepherd will permit the attack only if, in the long term, the pain is worth the gain.

The purpose of this test is to provide a testimony for the church.

Jesus was allowing Peter to experience a trial so he could encourage his brothers. Perhaps God is doing the same with you. God knows that the church needs living testimonies of his power. Your difficulty, your disease, your conflict are preparing you to be a voice of encouragement to your brothers. All you need to remember is that:

> No test or temptation that comes your way is beyond the course of what others have had to face. All you need to remember is that God will never let you down; he'll never let you be pushed past your limit; he'll always be there to help you come through it. (1 Cor. 10:13 MSG)

> "You meant evil against me; but God meant it for good." (Gen. 50:20 NKJV)

Remember, Satan cannot penetrate the walls of the Great House of God.

Is it still hard to imagine how your struggle could lead to any good? Still hard to conceive how your disease or debt or death could be a tool for anything worthwhile? If so, then I've got one final example. While not wanting to minimize your struggle, I must say yours is a cakewalk compared to this one. A sinless Savior was covered with sin. The Author of Life was placed in the cave of death. Satan's victory appeared sure. Finally the devil had scored on the right end of the court. And not only had he scored; he'd slam-dunked the MVP and left him lying on the floor. The devil had blown it with everyone from Sarah to Peter, but this time he'd done it right. The whole world had seen it. The victory dance had already begun.

But all of a sudden there was a light in the tomb and a rumbling of the rock; then Friday's tragedy emerged as Sunday's Savior, and even Satan knew he'd been had. He'd been a tool in the hand of the

Gardener. All the time he thought he was defeating heaven, he was helping heaven. God wanted to prove his power over sin and death, and that's exactly what he did. And guess who helped him do it? Once again Satan's layup becomes a foul-up. Only this time, he didn't give heaven some points, he gave heaven the championship game.

Jesus emerged as the victor, and Satan was left looking like a . . . well, I'll let you figure that out. Take the first letter of each of the ways God uses the devil and see if you can find Satan's true identity.

Refine the faithful.

Awaken the sleeping.

Teach the church.

CHAPTER 14

There are some mountains we should never go at

THE CHAPEL

RELYING ON GOD'S POWER

For thine is the kingdom, and the power, and the glory, for ever. Amen.

I came across an article about a lady who reminds me of us. She went up a mountain she should have avoided. No one would have blamed her had she stayed behind. At twelve below zero, even Frosty the Snowman would have opted for the warm fire. Hardly a day for snow skiing, but her husband insisted, and she went.

While waiting in the lift line, she realized she was in need of a restroom, dire need of a restroom. Assured there would be one at the top of the lift, she and her bladder endured the bouncy ride, only to find there was no facility. She began to panic. Her husband had an idea: Why not go into the woods? Since she was wearing an all-white outfit, she'd blend in with the snow. And what better powder room than a piney grove?

What choice did she have? She skied past the tree line and arranged her ski suit at half-mast. Fortunately, no one could see her. Unfortunately, her husband hadn't told her to remove her skis. Before you could say, "Shine on harvest moon," she was streaking backward

Mountains, ⟨ Kingdom
we should not ⟨ Power
climb   ⟨ Glory

across the slope, revealing more about herself than she ever intended. (After all, hindsight is 20/20.) With arms flailing and skis sailing, she sped under the very lift she'd just ridden and collided with a pylon.

As she scrambled to cover the essentials, she discovered her arm was broken. Fortunately her husband raced to her rescue. He summoned the ski patrol, who transported her to the hospital.

While being treated in the emergency room, a man with a broken leg was carried in and placed next to her. By now she'd regained her composure enough to make small talk. "So, how'd you break your leg?" she asked.

"It was the darndest thing you ever saw," he explained. "I was riding up the ski lift and suddenly I couldn't believe my eyes. There was this crazy woman skiing backwards, at top speed. I leaned over to get a better look and I guess I didn't realize how far I'd moved. I fell out of the lift."

Then he turned to her and asked, "So how'd you break your arm?"[1]

Don't we make the same mistake? We climb mountains we were never intended to climb. We try to go up when we should have stayed down, and as a result, we've taken some nasty spills in full view of a watching world. The tale of the lady (sorry, I couldn't resist) echoes our own story. There are certain mountains we were never made to climb. Ascend them and you'll end up bruised and embarrassed. Stay away from them and you'll sidestep a lot of stress. These mountains are described in the final phrase of the Lord's Prayer, "Thine is the kingdom and the power and the glory forever. Amen."

A RETURN TO THE CHAPEL

Our Lord's prayer has given us a blueprint for the Great House of God. From the living room of our Father to the family room with our friends, we are learning why David longed to "live in the house of the

LORD forever" (Ps. 23:6). In God's house we have everything we need: a solid foundation, an abundant table, sturdy walls, and an impenetrable roof of grace.

And now, having seen every room and explored each corner, we have one final stop. Not to a new room but to one we have visited earlier. We return to the chapel. We return to the room of worship. The chapel, remember, is where we stand before God and confess, "Hallowed be thy name."

The chapel is the only room in the house of God we visit twice. It's not hard to see why. It does us twice as much good to think about God as it does to think about anyone or anything else. God wants us to begin and end our prayers thinking of him. Jesus is urging us to look at the peak more than we look at the trail. The more we focus up there, the more inspired we are down here.

Some years ago a sociologist accompanied a group of mountain climbers on an expedition. Among other things, he observed a distinct correlation between cloud cover and contentment. When there was no cloud cover and the peak was in view, the climbers were energetic and cooperative. When the gray clouds eclipsed the view of the mountaintop, though, the climbers were sullen and selfish.

The same thing happens to us. As long as our eyes are on his majesty, there is a bounce in our step. But let our eyes focus on the dirt beneath us, and we will grumble about every rock and crevice we have to cross. For this reason Paul urged, "Don't shuffle along, eyes to the ground, absorbed with the things right in front of you. Look up, and be alert to what is going on around Christ—that's where the action is. See things from *his* perspective" (Col. 3:1–2 MSG).

Paul challenges you to "be alert to the things going on around Christ." The psalmist reminds you to do the same; only he used a different phrase. "O magnify the LORD with me, and let us exalt his name together" (Ps. 34:3 KJV).

Magnify. What a wonderful verb to describe what we do in the

Matt. 6

chapel. When you magnify an object, you enlarge it so that you can understand it. When we magnify God, we do the same. We enlarge our awareness of him so we can understand him more. This is exactly what happens in the chapel of worship—we take our mind off ourselves and set it on God. The emphasis is on him. "Thine is the kingdom and the power and the glory forever." *Term of respect to the Lord.*

And this is exactly the purpose of this final phrase in the Lord's Prayer. These words magnify the character of God. I love the way this phrase is translated in *The Message*:

"You're in charge!

You can do anything you want!

You're ablaze in beauty!

Yes! Yes! Yes!"

Could it be any simpler? God is in charge! This concept is not foreign to us. When the restaurant waiter brings you a cold hamburger and a hot soda, you want to know who is in charge. When a young fellow wants to impress his girlfriend, he takes her down to the convenience store where he works and boasts, "Every night from five to ten o'clock, I'm in charge." We know what it means to be in charge of a restaurant or a store, but to be in charge of the universe? This is the claim of Jesus.

> God raised him from death and set him on a throne in deep heaven, *in charge* of running the universe, everything from galaxies to governments, no name and no power exempt from his rule. And not just for the time being, but forever. He is *in charge* of it all, has the final word on everything. At the center of all this, Christ rules the church. (Eph. 1:22–23 MSG, emphasis mine)

There are many examples of Jesus' authority, but I'll just mention one of my favorites. Jesus and the disciples are in a boat crossing the

Sea of Galilee. A storm arises suddenly, and what was placid becomes violent—monstrous waves rise out of the sea and slap the boat. Mark described it clearly: "A furious squall came up, and the waves broke over the boat, so that it was nearly swamped" (Mark 4:37 NIV).

It's very important that you get an accurate picture, so I'm going to ask you to imagine yourself in the boat. It's a sturdy vessel but no match for these ten-foot waves. It plunges nose first into the wall of water. The force of the waves dangerously tips the boat until the bow seems to be pointing straight at the sky, and just when you fear flipping over backward, the vessel pitches forward into the valley of another wave. A dozen sets of hands join yours in clutching the mast. All your shipmates have wet heads and wide eyes. You tune your ear for a calming voice, but all you hear are screams and prayers. All of a sudden it hits you—someone is missing. Where is Jesus? He's not at the mast. He's not grabbing the edge. Where is he? Then you hear something—a noise . . . a displaced sound . . . like someone is snoring. You turn and look, and there curled in the stern of the boat is Jesus, sleeping!

You don't know whether to be amazed or angry, so you're both. How can he sleep at a time like this? Or as the disciples asked, "Teacher, don't you care if we drown?" (Mark 4:38 NIV).

If you're a parent of a teenager, you've been asked similar questions. The time you refused to mortgage your house so your daughter could buy the latest style tennis shoes, she asked, "Don't you care if I look out-of-date?"

When you insisted that your son skip the weekend game and attend his grandparents' golden anniversary, he asked, "Don't you care if I have a social life?"

When you limited the ear piercing to one hole per lobe, the accusation came thinly veiled as a question, "Don't you care if I fit in?"

Do the parents care? Of course they do. It's just that they have a different perspective. What the teenager sees as a storm, mom and dad see as a spring shower. They've been around enough to know these things pass.

So had Jesus. The very storm that made the disciples panic made him drowsy. What put fear in their eyes put him to sleep. The boat was a tomb to the followers and a cradle to Christ. How could he sleep through the storm? Simple, he was in charge of it.

The same happens with you and televisions. Ever doze off with the TV on? Of course you have. But put the same television in the grass hut of a primitive Amazonian Indian who has never seen one and, believe me, he won't sleep. How could anyone sleep in the presence of a talking box! As far as he knows, those little people behind the glass wall might climb out of the box and come after him. There is no way he's going to sleep. And there is no way he's going to let you sleep either. If you doze off, he'll wake you up. Don't you care that we're about to be massacred? Rather than argue with him, what do you do? You just point the remote at the screen and turn it off.

Jesus didn't even need a remote. "He got up, rebuked the wind and said to the waves, 'Quiet! Be still!' Then the wind died down, and it was completely calm. He said to his disciples, 'Why are you so afraid? Do you still have no faith?'" (Mark 4:39–40 NIV).

Incredible. He doesn't chant a mantra or wave a wand. No angels are called; no help is needed. The raging water becomes a stilled sea, instantly. Immediate calm. Not a ripple. Not a drop. Not a gust. In a moment the sea goes from a churning torrent to a peaceful pond. The reaction of the disciples? Read it in verse 41: "They were in absolute awe, staggered. 'Who is this, anyway?' they asked. 'Wind and sea at his beck and call!'" (MSG).

They'd never met a man like this. The waves were his subjects, and the winds were his servants. And that was just the beginning of what his sea mates would witness. Before it was over, they would see fish jump into the boat, demons dive into pigs, cripples turn into dancers, and cadavers turn into living, breathing people. "He even gives orders to evil spirits and they obey him," the people proclaimed (Mark 1:27 NIV).

Is it any wonder the disciples were willing to die for Jesus? Never had they seen such power, never had they seen such glory. It was like, well, like the whole universe was his kingdom. You wouldn't have needed to explain this verse to them; they knew what it meant: "Thine is the kingdom and the power and the glory forever."

In fact, it was two of these rescued fishermen who would declare his authority most clearly. Listen to John: "Greater is he that is in you, than he that is in the world" (1 John 4:4 KJV). Listen to Peter: "Jesus has gone into heaven and is at God's right side ruling over angels, authorities, and powers" (1 Pet. 3:22).

It's only right that they declare his authority. And it's only right that we do the same. And that is exactly what this phrase is, a declaration. A declaration of the heart. A declaration God deserves to hear. Doesn't he? Doesn't he deserve to hear us proclaim his authority? Isn't it right for us to shout from the bottom of our hearts and at the top of our voice, "Thine is the kingdom and the power and the glory forever!" Isn't it right for us to stare at these mountain peaks of God and worship him?

Of course it is. Not only does God deserve to hear our praise, but we also need to give it.

Mountains You Weren't Made to Climb

There are certain mountains only God can climb. The names of these mountains? You'll see them as you look from the window of the chapel in the Great House of God. "Thine is the kingdom and the power and the glory forever." A trio of peaks mantled by the clouds. Admire them, applaud them, but don't climb them.

It's not that you aren't welcome to try; it's just that you aren't able. The pronoun is *thine*, not *mine*; *thine* is the kingdom, not *mine* is the kingdom. If the word *Savior* is in your job description, it's because you put it there. Your role is to help the world, not save it. Mount Messiah is one mountain you weren't made to climb.

Nor is Mount Self-Sufficient. You aren't able to run the world, nor are you able to sustain it. Some of you think you can. You are self-made. You don't bow your knees; you just roll up your sleeves and put in another twelve-hour day . . . which may be enough when it comes to making a living or building a business. But when you face your own grave or your own guilt, your power will not do the trick.

You were not made to run a kingdom, nor are you expected to be all-powerful. And you certainly can't handle all the glory. Mount Applause is the most seductive of the three peaks. The higher you climb, the more people applaud, but the thinner the air becomes. More than one person has stood at the top and shouted, "Mine is the glory!" only to lose their balance and fall.

"Thine is the kingdom and the power and the glory forever." What protection this final phrase affords. As you confess that God is in charge, you admit that you aren't. As you proclaim that God has power, you admit that you don't. And as you give God all the applause, there is none left to dizzy your brain.

Let's let the lady on the slope teach us a lesson: There are certain mountains we weren't meant to climb. Stay below where you were made to be, so you won't end up exposing yourself to trouble.

CHAPTER 15

A HOME FOR YOUR HEART

My daughter Sara had a friend over to spend the night recently. There was no school the next day, so we let the two of them stay up as late as they wanted. A bedtime reprieve for a couple of seven-year-olds is like freeing a convict from death row. The two outlasted me. I was dozing in my chair when I awoke and realized it was nearly midnight and they were still awake. "All right, girls," I informed them, "we better go to bed." Groaning the entire time, they changed clothes, brushed their teeth, and climbed in the sack. That's when our little guest asked to call her mom. At first we declined, but then the chin trembled, and the eyes misted, and, knowing we were moments away from an explosion, we gave her the phone.

I could envision what was happening on the other end of the line—a phone ringing in the dark, a mom reaching over the slumbering husband to grab the receiver.

The little girl didn't even say hello. "Mommy, I want to come home." With a teddy bear in one hand and the phone in the other, she pleaded her case. She was afraid of waking up in a strange room. This wasn't her house. She wanted her bed, her pillow, and most of all, her mommy.

I can't blame her. When I travel, the hardest part of the trip is going to sleep. The pillow never feels right, the sheets are too . . . too stiff? Besides, who knows who slept there last night. The curtains never block the flashing neon light outside the window. I need to get up early, but can I trust the operator to remember the wake-up call? After all, there was that night in Boise when no one called me and . . . off go my thoughts, covering every issue from Denalyn's doctor visit to tomorrow's flight to next spring's income tax. I'd call home, but it's too late. I'd go for a walk, but I might get mugged. I'd order room service, but I already have. I'd go home, but, well, I'm supposed to be a grown man. Finally, I sit up in bed and flip on the TV and watch Sports Center until my eyes burn, then eventually doze off.

I can relate to Sara's friend. When it comes to resting your body, there's no house like your own.

I can also relate to the psalmist, David. When it comes to resting your soul, there is no place like the Great House of God. "I'm asking GOD for one thing," he wrote, "only one thing: to live with him in his house my whole life long. I'll contemplate his beauty; I'll study at his feet. That's the only quiet, secure place in a noisy world" (Ps. 27:4–5 MSG).

If you could ask God for one thing, what would you request? David tells us what he would ask. He longed to *live* in the house of God. I emphasize the word *live* because it deserves to be emphasized. David didn't want to chat. He didn't desire a cup of coffee on the back porch. He didn't ask for a meal or to spend an evening in God's house. He wanted to move in with him . . . forever. He was asking for his own room . . . permanently. He didn't want to be stationed in God's house, he longed to retire there. He didn't seek a temporary assignment but rather lifelong residence.

When David said, "I will dwell in the house of the LORD forever" (Ps. 23:6 NKJV), he was saying simply that he never wanted to step away from God. He craved to remain in the aura, in the atmosphere, in the awareness that he is in God's house, wherever he is.

The Lord's Prayer is a floor plan of the house of God: a step-by-step description of how God meets our needs when we dwell in him. Everything that occurs in a healthy house is described in this prayer. Protection, instruction, forgiveness, provision . . . all occur under God's roof.

"Then why," you might ask, "don't more people feel protected, forgiven, or instructed?"

My answer is as simple as the question is direct. Most have not learned to dwell in the house. Oh, we visit it. We stop in for the day or even drop by for a meal. But abide here? This is God's desire.

Remember the promise of his Son, "If people love me, they will obey my teaching. My Father will love them, and we will come to them and make our home with them" (John 14:23). He wants to be the one in whom "we live and move and have our being" (Acts 17:28 NIV).

Let me conclude with an example of how this prayer can be a home for your heart. I have a long way to go, but I'm trying to learn to dwell in the Great House of God. Over the last seven days I took note of the times I took strength from a part of the house.

On Monday I was tired, physically drained, so I stepped into the chapel and said, "Thine is the power," and the Father reminded me it was okay to rest.

On Tuesday I had more to do than I had hours to do it. Rather than stress out, I stepped into the kitchen and asked for daily bread. He gave me the strength to get everything done.

On Wednesday I was in the kitchen again. Needing some ideas for a children's book, I stepped up to the table and made a request. By bedtime the manuscript was drafted.

We had a strategic staff meeting this week. We began with a half hour of prayer and worship during which I stepped into the observatory and then into the chapel. I asked the God who made the heavens to make sure the meeting went well, and he did. I asked the holy God who is above us to guide us, and he did.

On one occasion I was impatient. I went into the hallway to ask for God's grace, only to find it already given. On another I was tempted, yet at just the right time a person entered the room with a word of wisdom, and I was reminded of the thickness of the wall. And then there was the frustration I felt over a person's opinion. Not knowing how to respond, I stepped into the study and opened the word, and 1 Corinthians 13:4 reminded me, "Love is patient and kind."

I don't want to leave the wrong impression. There were times when I worried rather than worshipped; there were times when I told God what I had to have rather than trust him to fill my plate. But day by day I'm learning to live in the Great House of God.

I hope you are too. Take Paul's advice and "pray without ceasing" (1 Thess. 5:17 NKJV). Make it your aim never to leave God's house. When you're worried about your bills, step into God's kitchen. When you feel bad about a mistake, look up at the roof. When you call on a new client, whisper a prayer as you enter the office: "Thy kingdom come to this place." When you're in a tense meeting, mentally step into the furnace room and pray, "Let the peace of heaven be felt on earth." When it's hard to forgive your spouse, pull out the check of grace God has given you.

My prayer for you is the same as Paul's: "Let your minds be remade and your whole nature thus transformed" (Rom. 12:2 NEB). May the Holy Spirit change your mind. May you grow so at ease in the house of God that you never leave it. And when you find yourself in another house, may you do what Sara's friend did—call home. Tell your Father that you can't rest in anyone's house but his. He won't mind the call. In fact, he'll be waiting by the phone.

Postscript

HIS MODEL, OUR GUIDE

We're home.

D oesn't it feel wonderful, knowing we're home where we belong? Here, in the place where our spirit has longed to rest . . . the place where we feel safe and secure.

Could I make a suggestion for your life in God's Great House? Each day, as you awaken in his presence, remember the blueprint. And as you talk to your Father, trace the floor plan in your mind. It's a helpful way to enter his presence. Here's an example of how the Lord's Prayer (Matt. 6:9–13 NASB) can guide your prayers:

Our Father
Thank you for adopting me into your family.
who is
Thank you, my Lord,
for being a God of the present tense:
my Jehovah-jireh (the God who provides),
my Jehovah-raah (the caring Shepherd),

my Jehovah-shalom (the Lord is peace),
my Jehovah-rophe (the God who heals),
and my Jehovah-nissi (Lord, my banner).
in heaven,
Your workshop of creation reminds me: If you can make the skies,
you can make sense out of my struggles.
Hallowed be your name.
Be holy in my heart.
You are "a cut above" all else.
Enable me to set my sights on you.
Your kingdom come.
Come, kingdom!
Be present, Lord Jesus!
Have free reign in every corner of my life.
Your will be done,
Reveal your heart to me, dear Father.
Show me my role in your passion.
Grant me guidance in the following decisions . . .
On earth as it is in heaven.
Thank you that you silence heaven to hear my prayer.
On my heart are the ones you love.
I pray for . . .
Give us this day our daily bread.
I accept your portion for my life today.
I surrender the following concerns
regarding my well-being . . .
And forgive us our debts,
I thank you for the roof of grace over my head,
bound together with the timbers and nails of Calvary. There is
nothing I can do to earn or add to your mercy.
I confess my sins to you . . .

as we also have forgiven our debtors.
Treat me, Father, as I treat others.
Have mercy on the following friends
who have wounded me . . .
And do not lead us into temptation . . .
Let my small hand be engulfed in yours.
Hold me, lest I fall.
I ask for special strength regarding . . .
Our Father . . . give us . . . forgive us . . . lead us . . .
Let your kindness be on all your church.
I pray especially for ministers near
and missionaries far away.
For Yours—not mine—is the kingdom
I lay my plans at your feet.
Yours—not mine—is the power
I come to you for strength.
Yours—not mine—is the glory
I give you all the credit.
forever. Amen.

NOTES

CHAPTER 2: THE LIVING ROOM

1. Joachim Jeremias, *The Prayers of Jesus* (New York: SCM Press, 1967), 57, as quoted in John Stott, "Has Anyone Told You About the Power of Prayer?" audiotape, All Souls Cassettes, No. E42/1A.

CHAPTER 3: THE FOUNDATION

1. All information on the names of God was taken from Nathan Stone, *Names of God* (Chicago: Moody Press, 1944).

CHAPTER 4: THE OBSERVATORY

1. Adapted from Brennan Manning, *The Ragamuffin Gospel* (Portland, OR: Multnomah Press, 1990), 32–33.

CHAPTER 9: THE KITCHEN

1. Source unknown.

2. Charles Panati, *Panati's Extraordinary Origins of Everyday Things* (New York: Harper & Row, 1987), 81.

3. Ibid., 86.

4. Alan Redpath, *Victorious Praying* (Grand Rapids, MI: Revell, 1973), 74.

CHAPTER 11: THE HALLWAY

1. John MacArthur, "The Pardon of Prayer" audio tape, © 1980 John MacArthur (Word of Grace, Panorama City, CA).

2. Thanks to Harold C. Staub for permission to use this letter.

CHAPTER 12: THE FAMILY ROOM

1. K. Hubbard, "A Gift of Grace: The Death of Conjoined Twins Ruth and Verena Cady," *People Weekly*, 5 November 1993, vol. 36, 42–44.

CHAPTER 13: THE WALLS

1. Erwin Lutzer, *The Serpent of Paradise* (Chicago: Moody Press, 1996), 102.

2. Ibid., 111.

CHAPTER 14: THE CHAPEL

1. Lois Lambley, ". . . so how'd you break your arm?" Et Cetera, *North Bend Eagle*, 18 January 1995, 4.

STUDY GUIDE

WRITTEN BY STEVE HALLIDAY

CHAPTER 1

❧

THE GREAT HOUSE OF GOD:
A HOME FOR YOUR HEART

LET US PONDER

1. God can be your dwelling place.

   A. *In what way can God be someone's dwelling place?*

   B. *Is God your dwelling place? Explain.*

2. You may go days without thinking of God, but there's never a moment when he's not thinking of you.

   A. *How often do you estimate that you think of God? What keeps you from thinking about him? How do you overcome this obstacle?*

   B. *Do you believe God never stops thinking about you? Explain.*

3. You are one step away from the house of God. Wherever you are. Whatever time it is.

   A. *What does Max mean by "stepping into the house of God"?*

   B. *Does this image of the Great House of God help you to grasp and utilize the Lord's Prayer? If so, how? If not, why not?*

4. Christ has provided more than a model for prayer, he has provided a model for living. These words do more than tell us what to say to God, they tell us how to exist with God.

   A. *In what way is the Lord's Prayer a model for living?*

   B. *How does the Lord's Prayer tell us how to exist with God?*

   C. *What part of the Lord's Prayer speaks most powerfully to you? Why?*

LET US PREPARE

1. Read through the Lord's Prayer in Matthew 6:9–13.

   A. *What part of this prayer most encourages you? Why?*

   B. *What part most convicts you? Why?*

   C. *Are there any parts you don't understand? If so, what are they? (Then especially look for Max's comments on that part later in the book.)*

   D. *If you were to assign parts of a house to each part of this prayer, how would you do it?*

2. Read Acts 17:24–28.

   A. *What picture of God does this passage portray? How does this picture fit into your concept of prayer? Explain.*

B. Note verse 28. How does the concept mentioned here fit with Max's image of the Great House of God?

3. Read Psalm 90:1–2.

A. What is significant about that?

B. What kind of requests does Moses make of God in the rest of this psalm? (See especially verses 12–17.)

4. Read 1 Thessalonians 5:17–18; Romans 12:12; Ephesians 6:18–20; Hebrews 13:15, 18–19; Colossians 4:2–4; Philippians 4:6–7.

A. What do you learn about prayer in each of the verses above?

5. How does the pattern of prayer laid out in the Lord's Prayer relate to the passages listed above?

LET US PRAY

1. This week read through the Lord's Prayer in Matthew 6:9–13 at least once each day. Read it meditatively to soak in its rich truth. Then take some time to pray about the concerns that touch your life, based on this pattern prayer.

2. Sit down with a piece of paper and a pen and "take apart" the Lord's Prayer phrase by phrase. Divide the prayer into units that make sense to you—"Our Father," for example, or "hallowed be thy name"—and write a paragraph on how that unit is significant to you. Then take a moment to "pray through" the whole prayer, especially considering what you have written about its various parts.

CHAPTER 2

THE LIVING ROOM: WHEN YOUR
HEART NEEDS A FATHER

LET US PONDER

1. You may be willing to stop being God's child. But God is not willing to stop being your Father.

   A. *Were you ever willing to stop being God's child? If so, explain. What would cause anyone to want to stop being his child?*

   B. *How do we know God is not willing to stop being our Father? How would you try to explain this to someone who thought it was too good to be true?*

2. "Our Father" reminds us we are welcome in God's house because we have been adopted by the owner.

A. *Do you feel welcome in God's house? If so, why? If not, why not?*

B. *What is significant about becoming a member of God's family through adoption? Why does the Bible use this term adopted?*

3. God adopted you simply because he wanted to. You were his good will and pleasure.

A. *Why do you think God would want to adopt any of us? What does he get out of the deal?*

B. *In what way are all believers (including you) God's "good will and pleasure"? Why does Max believe this? Do you believe it? Explain.*

4. Our God is no fair-weather Father. He's not into this love-'em-and-leave-'em stuff. I can count on him to be in my corner no matter how I perform. You can too.

A. *Why is it important to know that God will never leave us? What does this knowledge do for us?*

B. *Do you always feel as though God is in your corner? What might account for these feelings? Are they true? How can we deal with them?*

LET US PREPARE

1. Consider the phrase "Our Father."

A. *What does this phrase communicate to you? How does it make you feel? What pictures does it bring to mind?*

B. *In what ways is God like a father?*

2. Read Luke 15:11–32.

    A. *What picture of a father is being presented in this story? Why do you think Jesus would paint such a picture?*

    B. *With which character in the story do you most closely identify? Why?*

    C. *Why is verse 20 an especially good picture of our heavenly Father? How can keeping this picture in mind help our prayer lives?*

3. Read Romans 8:15–17; Galatians 4:4–7; Ephesians 1:3–8.

    A. *According to these passages, how does someone become a child of God?*

    B. *What rights and privileges are granted to God's children, according to these verses?*

    C. *How do you think this knowledge is supposed to affect our prayer lives? Does it influence the way you pray? Why or why not?*

LET US PRAY

1. Spend at least five minutes alone with God, speaking to him about nothing other than what it means to you to be called his child.

2. Get out a concordance and find several of the more than 200 times God is called "Father" in the New Testament. Choose ten of these texts and pray through them, speaking to God about his fatherly characteristics as described in the verses you chose.

CHAPTER 3

THE FOUNDATION: WHERE TRUST BEGINS

LET US PONDER

1. God is the foundation of his own house.

   A. *What does it mean that God is the foundation of his own house?*

   B. *How stable would the house be if God were not its foundation? Explain.*

   C. *What would happen if God's house were built on the foundation of your own strength? Do we ever act as though this were true? Explain.*

2. The key question in life is not "How strong am I?" but rather "How strong is God?"

A. Why is this the key question in life?

B. Why is it so easy to reverse the above statements? Do you ever do this? If so, what happens?

C. This key question depends on your relationship to God. Explain why this is so, and describe how you came into a relationship with him. How would you describe that relationship?

3. Meditating on the names of God reminds you of the character of God. Take these names and bury them in your heart.

A. Max lists several of God's names. Which one means the most to you? Why?

B. How does one bury the names of God in one's heart? What does this mean? Why is it important? Have you done this? Explain.

LET US PREPARE

1. Consider the phrase "Our Father who is."

A. What does it mean to you that God is?

B. How would you feel if God wasn't?

C. How does God show you, personally, that he is?

2. Read Isaiah 6:1–4 and Revelation 4:6–11.

A. What attribute of God is most prominent in these two passages? Describe this trait in your own words.

B. How do those who surround God as described in these passages respond to him? Why do they so respond?

C. *Why is it important to keep these thoughts in mind when we address our heavenly Father in prayer?*

3. Consider the following Scriptures that give various names of God. How is each one important? For each one, identify what life circumstances would make that trait especially appealing:

A. *Genesis 1:1, Elohim (God the Creator).*

B. *Genesis 48:15, Jehovah-raah (Caring Shepherd).*

C. *Genesis 22:7–8, Jehovah-jireh (The Lord who Provides).*

D. *Judges 6:24, Jehovah-shalom (The Lord is Peace).*

E. *Exodus 15:26, Jehovah-rophe (The Lord who Heals You).*

F. *Exodus 17:8–16, Jehovah-nissi (The Lord my Banner).*

Let Us Pray

1. Take a few moments to confess to God your weakness. Be specific—for example, confess your short temper or your pride or your devotion to things rather than people. Then take at least twice as long to praise God for his strength and faithfulness to you. Thank him for cleansing you through the blood of his Son and for adopting you into his family.

2. Pick one of the names of God listed above and meditate on that name for an entire day. Write the appropriate verse on a card and refer to it frequently throughout the day. Then, before you retire for the night, praise God for showing that trait to you and thank him for acting according to his name.

CHAPTER 4

❧❦❧

THE OBSERVATORY:
A HEAVENLY AFFECTION

LET US PONDER

1. God dwells in a different realm. He occupies a different
dimension.

   A. *In what way does God dwell in a different realm and different
   dimension from us?*

   B. *If God does not dwell with us, how can he be of help to us?*

2. You want to know who God is? See what he has done.

   A. *Do you want to know who God is? Why or why not? What difference does it make?*

   B. *How does seeing what God has done show us who he is? From
   what you see, who would you say God is? Explain.*

3. Spend some time walking in the workshop of the heavens, seeing what God has done, and watch how your prayers are energized.

A. *Why does Max think there is a connection between gazing at the stars and the strength of one's prayer life? Is this connection present in your life? Explain.*

B. *When was the last time you spent several minutes just observing the heavens? Could you do so tonight?*

4. Next time a sunrise steals your breath or a meadow of flowers leaves you speechless, remain that way. Say nothing and listen as heaven whispers, "Do you like it? I did it just for you."

A. *Why is silence often an appropriate response to the feeling of wonder?*

B. *Do you think God would have made the world so beautiful if you were the only one on the planet? Explain.*

Let Us Prepare

1. Consider the phrase "Our Father who is in heaven."

A. *Does the fact that God is in heaven make him feel distant to you at times? Explain.*

B. *What benefits are there in having a God in heaven?*

2. Read 1 Corinthians 1:25.

A. *What comparison is made in this verse? What is it intended to convey?*

B. *How should this verse give us great confidence in prayer?*

3. Read Isaiah 55:8–9.

    A. *What comparison is made in this verse? What is it intended to convey?*

    B. *Why should this verse give us great confidence in prayer?*

    C. *How can this verse help to explain some of our disappointments in prayer?*

4. Read Psalm 19:1–6.

    A. *How does the universe teach us about God, according to this passage?*

5. What did David learn about God from observing the universe? Do you think this knowledge helped or hindered his prayer life? Explain.

LET US PRAY

1. The next cloudless night, take a half hour to do nothing but lie on the ground and gaze up at the sky. What do you see? Try counting the stars. After you have basked in the glory of the heavens for a while, spend an equal amount of time praising God for what you have just seen. Praise him for his power, for his wisdom, for his grace and his love. Thank him that you have eyes to see his creation and a mind to comprehend some of it. Focus on his glory and majesty and splendor and might. Have a good time of celebrating God Almighty!

2. Take a few minutes to read through Revelation 21–22:6. Remember that the place this passage describes is God's home

and is merely a reflection of his majesty and greatness. Then praise him for creating such a beautiful place where we will spend eternity with him. Pray through this passage, thanking him for his goodness in providing such a marvelous eternal home for us.

CHAPTER 5

THE CHAPEL: WHERE MAN
COVERS HIS MOUTH

Let Us Ponder

1. There are times when to speak is to violate the moment . . .
   when silence represents the highest respect. The word for such
   times is *reverence*. The prayer for such times is "Hallowed be thy
   name."

   A. *What does* reverence *mean to you? Why is it associated with
   silence?*

   B. *How does one hallow God's name? From the opposite viewpoint,
   how does one profane it? In the last week, did you do more of one
   than the other? Explain.*

2. God says to Job, "As soon as you are able to handle these simple
   matters of storing stars and stretching the neck of the ostrich,

then we'll have a talk about pain and suffering. But till then, we can do without your commentary."

A. *If you had been in Job's shoes, do you think you would have reacted much as he did? Why or why not?*

B. *In times of trouble, do you ever demand answers of God? If he were to respond to your questions, what do you think he'd say?*

3. When you set your sights on God, you focus on One who is "a cut above" any storm life may bring.

A. *How can you set your sights on God? What does this entail?*

B. *How does setting one's sights on God help us in the middle of life's storms? Do you have any personal examples of this? If so, describe them.*

LET US PREPARE

1. Consider the phrase "hallowed be thy name."

A. *How does a person hallow something?*

B. *How does the term hallow relate to the term holy?*

2. Read Job 38:3–18.

A. *What is the point of all of God's questions? What lesson does he want Job to learn?*

B. *If you were in Job's shoes at this point in the story, how do you think you would react? Why?*

C. *What do you learn about God in this passage?*

3. Read Job 40:4–5; 42:1–6.

   A. *How did Job react to God's speeches? Was this an appropriate response? Why?*

   B. *What did Job finally learn about God? How did it change his attitude toward his circumstances?*

   C. *In all of God's speeches, does he answer Job's questions? What is significant about this?*

4. Read Psalm 46:10.

   A. *What command are we given in this verse? What is the reason for the command?*

   B. *Is this an easy command for you to obey? Why or why not? Why is it so crucial? What do we miss when we ignore it?*

LET US PRAY

1. Go for a long, leisurely walk someplace where you can be alone with God to enjoy the work of his hands. Be silent as you marvel at his handiwork and creativity. Notice everything you can around you—the colors, the smells, the shapes, the immensity and the smallness of his creation. Then at the end of your walk, break your silence and thank him both for the beauty of his creation and for the ability to walk and take it all in. Speak to him reverently and lovingly, trying to avoid making any requests during your prayer.

2. Slowly and carefully read through Job 38–41. Try to picture as much as you can of all the mysteries God describes. Then also

try to put yourself in Job's place—how would you feel if God should deliver such a power-packed message to you? Spend some time alone with God, in silence, basking in his overwhelming majesty and splendor.

CHAPTER 6

THE THRONE: TOUCHING
THE KING'S HEART

LET US PONDER

1. When you say, "thy kingdom come," you are inviting the Messiah himself to walk into your world. . . . This is no feeble request; it's a bold appeal for God to occupy every corner of your life.

   A. *Have you ever invited the Messiah to walk into your world? If so, how? If not, why not?*

   B. *Does God "occupy every corner of your life" right now? Explain. If not, would you like him to? Explain.*

2. For Haman, the massacre is a matter of expediency. For Satan, it is a matter of survival. He will do whatever it takes to impede the presence of Jesus in the world.

A. Why was Satan's plan to wipe out the ancient Jews "a matter of survival"? What did he have at stake?

B. How do you think Satan tries to impede the presence of Jesus in the world today? How does he do it in your own corner of the world?

3. When we pray for God's kingdom to come, it comes! All the hosts of heaven rush to our aid.

A. If God's kingdom were to come into your workplace, what would happen?

B. In what way do the hosts of heaven rush to our aid when we pray for God's kingdom to come? Have you ever prayed for his kingdom to come, and this didn't seem to happen? Explain. What might we conclude from this?

LET US PREPARE

1. Consider the phrase "thy kingdom come."

A. When you think of God's coming kingdom, what comes to mind?

B. Why do you think we should pray that God's kingdom would come?

2. Read Esther 3–9.

A. What was the calamity facing God's people? Who engineered it? How did he engineer it?

B. How did God take these terrible circumstances and turn them on their heads? How did what was bad turn into what was good?

C. *What part did Esther play in this drama? What part did Mordecai play? What was the role of the king? From the text's point of view, who is the central character?*

D. *Choose one key verse for each of these seven chapters. Why do you think the verses you chose are significant? What do they teach you?*

E. *Note that Esther is the only book in the Bible that does not mention God by name. Can you see him in this book anyway? Explain.*

3. Read Hebrews 4:14–16.

A. *What title is Jesus given in this passage? What does this title tell us about his work on our behalf?*

B. *What reasons does this passage give us for trusting that Jesus can and will help us (see especially verse 15)?*

C. *What conclusion is made in verse 16, based on what is said in verses 14–15? Do you take advantage of this? Why or why not?*

4. Read Hebrews 12:28.

A. *What kind of kingdom are we to receive? How is this significant?*

B. *What is to be our response to this promise?*

C. *How is God described in this verse? Do you often think of him this way? Explain.*

LET US PRAY

1. Get a concordance and look up the word *kingdom* in the Gospel of Matthew (there are more than fifty references). Then take your Bible and read through each of these verses, trying to get a

"bird's-eye view" of the kingdom of God. As you read, frequently stop to pray about what you are learning. Remember, you are praying to the King of the kingdom!

2. Spend some time asking God to occupy every corner of your life. What *corners* might you still be withholding from him? Finances? Relationships? Work? School? Recreation? Be as honest with yourself as possible and take inventory of your life. Then invite the King to take control in every area.

CHAPTER 7

THE STUDY: HOW GOD
REVEALS HIS WILL

Let Us Ponder

1. God has a plan, and that plan is good. Our initial question is, how do I access it?

   A. *Do you believe God has a plan for you? If so, why? If not, why not?*

   B. *How do you access God's plan for your own life?*

2. To pray, "thy will be done" is to seek the heart of God.

   A. *Why does praying "thy will be done" indicate that we're seeking the heart of God? How is this prayer to change us?*

   B. *If you had to describe the heart of God to a non-Christian, what would you say?*

3. God's *general* will provides us with guidelines that help us understand his *specific* will for our individual lives.

   A. *What does Max mean by God's general will? What does he mean by God's specific will?*

   B. *How does God's general will help us to discover God's specific will? How do the two wills interrelate? Do you think his specific will ever contradicts or ignores his general will? Explain.*

4. Want to know God's will for your life? Then answer this question: "What ignites your heart?" . . . The fire of your heart is the light of your path. Disregard it at your own expense.

   A. *Do you want to know God's will for your life? If he were to tell you specifically and audibly right now what his will for you is, would you be willing to do it, no matter what? Explain.*

   B. *What ignites your own heart? What fills you with enthusiasm? Do you see how that interest can be translated into God's will for your life? Are there any cautions you should observe with this advice? If so, what?*

LET US PREPARE

1. Consider the phrase "thy will be done."

   A. *What do you already know about the will of God for you? Do you struggle with any part of it? Explain.*

   B. *Is it easy or hard for you to submit yourself to the will of God? Explain.*

2. Max lists four components that work together to help us find God's will:

· The people of God.

· The Word of God.

· Our walk with God.

· The fire of God.

In your own words, explain how each of these components "works."

Which of these components do you utilize most frequently? Which do you tend to overlook? What, if anything, needs to change so that all four can work together for you to find God's will?

3. Read Luke 24:13–35.

A. *What were the two men talking about as they walked to Emmaus? How would you describe their demeanor?*

B. *How did Jesus approach the men? Why do you think he approached them like this, and not more directly?*

C. *How did the men finally recognize Jesus? Is there anything significant about this? If so, what?*

D. *How did the men respond to their encounter? In what way is this a model for us?*

4. Read Matthew 7:21, 10:29; John 6:40; Acts 18:21; Romans 12:2; Ephesians 5:17–21; 1 Thessalonians 4:3–8, 5:18.

A. *What do you learn about God's will from these passages?*

B. *How eager are you to do the will of God he has already revealed to you? Take time to ask him to help you fulfill his will, whatever it may be for you.*

LET US PRAY

1. Get out a concordance and look up the word *will*, looking especially for those verses that tell us something about the will of God. Make a list of the items that are specially mentioned as being God's will for all of his children. Then spend some time praying about this list, thanking God for helping you to fulfill his will in those areas in which you are doing well, and asking him for his strength in those areas in which you struggle.

2. Many times we do not know exactly what God's will might be for us; we must follow the Lord's example in the Garden of Gethsemane by telling the Lord our request, then concluding our prayer by asking that "nevertheless, not my will, but your will be done." If there is some issue in your life that fits this model, pray about it right now.

CHAPTER 8

THE FURNACE: BECAUSE
SOMEONE PRAYED

LET US PONDER

1. The power of God was triggered by prayer. Jesus looked down
the very throat of death's cavern and called Lazarus back to
life . . . all because someone prayed.

   A. *Why do you think prayer often triggers the power of God? Why
   does this connection exist?*

   B. *What do you think might have happened in the case of Lazarus
   had someone not told Jesus about his friend's condition? Explain.*

2. The power of prayer does not depend on the one who makes the
prayer but on the One who hears the prayer.

A. Do you think Max is right about that statement? Why or why not?

B. Does the character of the person who prays have no bearing on the power of the prayer? Explain.

3. One call and heaven's fleet appears. Your prayer on earth activates God's power in heaven, and "God's will is done on earth as it is in heaven."

A. What would your neighborhood look like if God's will were done there as it is in heaven? What would your home look like? What part, if any, do you play in seeing this happen?

B. If it is true that "one call and heaven's fleet appears," then why do you think the Bible so often instructs us to pray "without ceasing"?

4. You are the someone of God's kingdom. You have access to God's furnace. Your prayers move God to change the world.

A. How often do you take advantage of your access to God's furnace? Are you satisfied with this? If not, what would it take for it to change?

B. Take a little time to discuss some of your prayers that helped change the world, at least, in your little corner of the planet.

LET US PREPARE

1. Consider the phrase "on earth as it is in heaven."

A. How is God's will done in heaven? Begrudgingly? Reluctantly? Complainingly? How do the angels do God's will?

B. *How do you usually do God's will on earth? Could it be said that you do his will as it is done in heaven? Explain.*

2. Read John 11:1–44.

A. *Retell the story in your own words.*

B. *How does Jesus respond when he hears of Lazarus's illness? Is this what you might have expected? Is it what his disciples expected? Explain.*

C. *How do Mary and Martha respond to Jesus when he finally comes to their town? How does he respond to them?*

D. *Why do you think Jesus waited to perform this miracle? (See especially verses 15, 40, and 42.)*

E. *What does this passage teach you about the will of God?*

3. Read Revelation 8:1–5.

A. *Describe what is happening in this passage.*

B. *Is any reason given for the silence of heaven in this passage? If so, what is it?*

C. *What do you learn about prayer in this passage?*

LET US PRAY

1. Get out a concordance and look up the word *hear* wherever it appears in the book of Psalms. Note how often the psalmists declare that God hears their prayers and how often they entreat him to hear. Using their prayers as a model, thank God for hearing you and bring to him any requests you may have.

2. Take stock of the areas of your life over which you exercise substantial control. If God's will is not being done in any of those areas as it would be done in heaven, ask God to help you rectify this. If these areas are going well, thank God for enabling you to do his will.

CHAPTER 9

THE KITCHEN: GOD'S ABUNDANT TABLE

LET US PONDER

1. God is not a mountain guru involved only in the mystical and spiritual. The same hand that guides your soul gives food for your body.

   A. *Do you know of anyone who thinks of God only as a "mountain guru"? If so, how do they respond to him? What do they do? What don't they do?*

   B. *Do you ever tend to think that the mystical and spiritual is more important (or more godly) than food for your body? Explain. What does God say about this?*

2. If you have followed Christ's model for prayer, your preoccupation has been his wonder rather than your stomach. The first three petitions are God-centered, not self-centered.

   A. *What does it mean to be preoccupied with God's wonder rather than your stomach? How does someone get to this point?*

   B. *What do you think Jesus was teaching in the Lord's Prayer by making the first three petitions God-centered rather than self-centered? Do your own prayers often follow this model? If not, why not?*

3. God lives with the self-assigned task of providing for his own, and so far, you've got to admit, he's done pretty well at the job.

   A. *How has God provided for you in this past week? In the past month? In the past year? Since you became a Christian?*

   B. *Does the knowledge that God promises to provide for you make a difference in the way you live? Why or why not?*

4. In the house of God, the One who provides the food is the One who prepares the meal.

   A. *What does Max mean in the statement above? What difference does it make?*

   B. *How has God prepared the meal for you? Describe at least one example.*

LET US PREPARE

1. Consider the phrase "Give us this day our daily bread."

A. *What do you think is included in the idea of daily bread?*

B. *Why do you think God tells us to ask every day for what we need that day?*

2. Review the two rules Max cites for asking God for our daily bread:

   · Don't be shy, ask.

   · Trust the cook.

   A. *Are you ever shy about asking God for something? If so, why?*

   B. *Why is it so important to "trust the cook"? How do we show that we sometimes don't trust the cook?*

3. Read Psalm 37:3–6.

   A. *What advice is given here about seeking our daily bread?*

   B. *What promise is given us here?*

4. Read Matthew 6:25–34.

   A. *What advice is given here about seeking our daily bread?*

   B. *What illustrations are given to help us understand God's ways?*

   C. *What promise is given to us if we will follow God's way?*

LET US PRAY

1. What special needs confront you today? List the pressing needs you have right now (not your special desires but your needs) and spend some unhurried time with your Lord, asking him to meet the specific needs you bring to him. Then thank him for hearing and trust that he will do what he says.

2. Note that the verse talks about "our" daily needs. What are some of the needs of your loved ones, colleagues, or close acquaintances? Make a list of these needs, and pray specifically that God would meet each one. When you are through praying, let these people know that you have been praying for them and ask them to let you know when God meets the need you've prayed about.

CHAPTER 10

❧✦❧

THE ROOF: BENEATH GOD'S GRACE

LET US PONDER

1. In God's house you are covered by the roof of his grace.

   A. *What does the term* grace *mean to you?*

   B. *How does grace cover you? In what way is a roof a good picture of grace? How has it sheltered you in the past week?*

2. If Christ had not covered us with his grace, each of us would be overdrawn on that account. When it comes to goodness we would have insufficient funds. Inadequate holiness.

   A. *Was there ever a time where you thought you had sufficient funds to cover your spiritual debts? If so, describe that time. What, if anything, convinced you that you were wrong?*

B. *How much holiness would we need to come into God's presence? How can we acquire such holiness?*

3. God assumed your debt. You assumed his fortune. And that's not all he did. He also paid your penalty.

A. *What does it mean that God assumed your debt? How was this done?*

B. *What does it mean that you assumed [God's] fortune? How was this done?*

C. *How did God pay your penalty?*

LET US PREPARE

1. Consider the phrase "Forgive us our debts."

A. *What debts have you owed to God? What does this term debts include?*

B. *Have you asked God to forgive your debts? If so, how? If not, why not?*

C. *How is God able to forgive us of our debts?*

2. Max develops two primary ideas in this chapter:

· We owe a debt we cannot pay.
· God paid a debt he did not owe.

A. *What is the debt we cannot pay? Why can we not pay it?*

B. *Why did God pay a debt he did not owe? How did he pay it?*

3. Read Isaiah 64:6 and Romans 3:23.

   A. *What do these verses tell us about our debt to God?*

   B. *What is the result of this debt?*

4. Read Romans 4:5, 8:33; 2 Corinthians 5:19–21; Galatians 3:13; 1 Peter 3:18.

   A. *How did God handle our debt, according to these verses?*

   B. *What, if anything, do these verses tell us we are required to do to take advantage of what God has done for us?*

LET US PRAY

1. Remind yourself of what Christ went through to provide redemption for us by reading the story of his Passion (Matthew 26:36–28:15; Mark 14:32–16:8; Luke 22:39–24:12; John 18:1–20:9). Take some time to thank him for his grace, especially recalling how he saved you from the just penalty of your own sins.

2. Be in prayer for others you know who do not yet know Christ, that they might also come to know the joy of God's forgiveness. Name these people specifically and ask that God might open a door for his children—perhaps you?—to share the gospel effectively with those who don't yet know him.

CHAPTER 11

THE HALLWAY: GRACE
RECEIVED, GRACE GIVEN

LET US PONDER

1. Dealing with debt is at the heart of your happiness. It's also at the heart of the Lord's Prayer.

   A. *Why is dealing with debt at the heart of a person's happiness?*

   B. *Why does Max say that debt is at the heart of the Lord's Prayer?*

   C. *How do you typically deal with debts owed to you?*

2. Confession does not create a relationship with God, it simply nourishes it.

   A. *Why does confession not create a relationship with God? If it doesn't create such a relationship, what does?*

B. *How does confession nourish a relationship with God? Is this easy or hard for you to do? Explain.*

3. In any given Christian community there are two groups: those who are contagious in their joy and those who are cranky in their faith.

   A. *Describe someone you know who is contagious in his or her joy.*

   B. *Describe someone you know (without naming the person!) who is cranky in his or her faith.*

   C. *Which type of Christian do you consider yourself? Would others agree?*

4. Want to enjoy God's generosity? Then let others enjoy yours.

   A. *How can you let others enjoy your generosity this week?*

   B. *If someone were to judge God's generosity by observing your own, what would they think?*

LET US PREPARE

1. Consider the phrase "Forgive us our debts as we also have forgiven our debtors."

   A. *This phrase troubles many people; why do you think it does? Does it trouble you? If so, why?*

   B. *Who are your debtors? Have you forgiven them? Explain.*

2. Max talks about "the high cost of getting even." What do the following texts tell us about this high cost?

   · Matthew 18:21–35

· Matthew 6:14–15

· Galatians 5:14–15

3. Read Luke 6:37–38.

A. What does this text tell us to avoid?

B. What does this text tell us to do?

C. What is the result of our obedience? What is the result of our disobedience?

Let Us Pray

1. Is there anyone in your life whom you have a hard time forgiving? If so, admit this to the Lord. Tell him about your feelings, without trying to justify why you feel that way. Ask him to give you his strength to do what you believe he is asking you to do: to forgive that person. Confess that this is not something you will be able to do on your own strength and that perhaps you even struggle with the desire to grant forgiveness to the person who hurt you. Commit this to the Lord and allow him to bring you to the place you need to be.

2. Is there anyone in your life who may be having a hard time forgiving you for something you have done? If so, ask the Lord to help you ask forgiveness of this person, no matter how hard it might be. After praying for God's strength and direction, approach the person and try to iron out your problems. Strive for peace.

CHAPTER 12

THE FAMILY ROOM: LEARNING
TO LIVE TOGETHER

LET US PONDER

1. We don't pray to *my* Father or ask for *my* daily bread or ask God
   to forgive *my* sins. In God's house we speak the language of plurality: *our* Father, *our* daily bread, *our* debts, *our* debtors, lead *us*
   not into temptation, and deliver *us*.

   A. *Why do you think Jesus stressed plurality in his prayer?*

   B. *Take stock of your own prayer life. Would you say it is more
   characterized by me prayers or us prayers? Explain.*

2. We all need a father . . . we are all beggars in need of bread . . .
   we are sinners in need of grace.

   A. *What is your most critical need from your Father? Why?*

B. What kind of bread do you most need today? Explain.

C. What form of grace do you most require right now? Why not ask God to supply it even at this moment?

3. In God's house we occasionally find ourselves next to people we don't like.

A. What kind of people do you find most difficult to get along with? Why? How do you deal with these folks?

B. Describe a time when you asked God to help you get along with someone you didn't like. What happened?

LET US PREPARE

1. Consider the term our.

A. Why do you think Jesus taught us to pray in the plural number rather than in the singular?

B. Do you make it a habit to pray for others as well as for yourself, or is this something you struggle with? Explain.

2. Max says we all need at least three things:

· We are children in need of a father.
· We are beggars in need of bread.
· We are sinners in need of grace.

A. In what ways has God shown himself to be a father to you?

B. In what ways do you recognize that you are a beggar in need of bread?

C. How do you show that you are a sinner in need of grace?

3. Read Romans 12:14–21.

   A. *What instruction does this text give us for living with others?*

   B. *What is the hardest thing in this passage for you to do? Why?*

4. Read Romans 14:10–13.

   A. *What general rule of thumb does Paul give us here for living with other believers? What is the reason behind this rule of thumb?*

   B. *What motivation does Paul give in verse 11 for obeying his instruction? Is this something you often think about? Should it be? Explain.*

LET US PRAY

1. Get together some evening with a few of your closest Christian friends and agree to pray for an hour—with one catch. Agree that each of you will pray for the others but that you will not pray for yourself.

2. Spend some time alone praying for the people and ministries of your church. Pray for guidance, for protection, for strength, for God's Spirit to lead you all into his love, truth, and service. Try not to pray much about yourself, but instead focus on the people who are growing in Christ with you at your church.

CHAPTER 13

❧❧❧

THE WALLS: SATAN, GOD'S SERVANT

LET US PONDER

1. Every time Satan sets out to score one for evil, he ends up scoring a point for good. When he schemes to thwart the kingdom, he always advances it.

   A. *Give a few biblical examples that illustrate the statements above.*

   B. *Describe a few incidents from your own life that demonstrated the truth of the statements above.*

2. Satan may strut and prance, but it's God who calls the shots.

   A. *How does Satan "strut and prance"? How does he do this in your own life?*

   B. *How important is it to know that God calls the shots? What practical difference does this make to the way we live?*

3. All angels, including Satan, are inferior to God. And, this may surprise you, Satan is still a servant to God.

   A. *Why is it important to know that angels are inferior to God? What would happen if they weren't?*

   B. *In what way is Satan a servant to God?*

4. The walls that surround the Great House of God—Satan cannot climb them; he cannot penetrate them. He has absolutely no power, except that power that God permits.

   A. *What are the walls that surround the Great House of God? Of what are they made?*

   B. *Why do you think God permits Satan any power at all?*

LET US PREPARE

1. Consider the phrase, "and lead us not into temptation, but deliver us from evil."

   A. *Why should we pray that God would not lead us into temptation? Is there really any danger of that? If not, what is the purpose of this part of the Lord's Prayer?*

   B. *In what ways has God delivered you from evil in the past year?*

2. Max says that God uses Satan in three primary ways:
   - To refine the faithful
   - To awaken the sleeping
   - To teach the church

   A. *How does Satan refine the faithful? How has he been used to refine you?*

B. How does Satan awaken the sleeping? Who are the sleeping? And how does he do this in your own experience?

C. Satan seems an unlikely teacher of the church. What does it mean that he can be used to teach the church? What lessons has your own church learned from him?

3. Read Isaiah 14:12–15 and Ezekiel 28:12–17.

A. What do these passages teach us about the transformation of Satan into an angel of darkness?

B. What was Satan's paramount sin, according to Ezekiel? How is this sin still a potent trap for us?

4. Read John 19:1–16.

A. From a human observer's point of view, who seems to be in control of this scene? Who is really in control? How do you know?

B. Note especially Jesus' words in verse 11. What does he tell Pilate? In what way are his words equally applicable to any of God's adopted children?

Let Us Pray

1. What are your biggest temptations in life? How do you handle them? Read 1 Corinthians 10:12–13; then ask God to give you the strength and the wisdom to handle in a godly way the temptations that come into your life. Ask him to help you remember that often the best course of action is to flee (2 Timothy 2:22) and to enable you to do what will bring him the most glory. Thank him for his protection and his watchful keeping over you.

2. Take some time to recall the many ways God has delivered you from evil since you became a Christian. Recount as many as you can think of, thanking God for his power and praising him for his strength and goodness. Then ask him to continue to deliver you from the temptations and trials that inevitably come your way.

CHAPTER 14

❧

THE CHAPEL: RELYING
ON GOD'S POWER

LET US PONDER

1. The chapel is the only room in the house of God we visit
   twice. . . . It does us twice as much good to think about God as
   it does to think about anyone or anything else. God wants us to
   begin and end our prayers thinking of him.

   A. *Why would God have us visit the chapel, and no other room,*
   twice? What is so special about the chapel?

   B. *Do you usually begin and end your prayers by thinking of God?*
   If not, how can you change your normal practice? And why
   should you?

2. As long as our eyes are on his majesty, there is a bounce in our step. But let our eyes focus on the dirt beneath us, and we will grumble about every rock and crevice we have to cross.

   A. *Why is there a bounce in our step when we gaze upon his majesty? Why does this energize us?*

   B. *What does it mean to "focus on the dirt beneath us"? Why is this so easy to do? How can we prompt ourselves to quit looking at dirt and start gazing at God?*

3. You were not made to run a kingdom, nor are you expected to be all-powerful. And you certainly can't handle all the glory.

   A. *How do we sometimes act as if we were made to run a kingdom? As if we were all-powerful?*

   B. *Why aren't we equipped to handle all the glory? If we're not, who is? And what makes him so different from us?*

4. As you confess that God is in charge, you admit that you aren't.

   A. *How easy is it for you to admit that God is in charge and you aren't? Explain.*

   B. *What are some practical ways to admit we're not in charge and to confess that God is?*

LET US PREPARE

1. Consider the phrase "For thine is the kingdom and the power and the glory. Amen."

   A. *In what way is this an appropriate ending to the Lord's Prayer?*

   B. *How do each of the three main terms—kingdom, power, and* glory—*focus our attention once more on God? What do each of these terms convey to you?*

2. Read Colossians 3:1–4.

   A. *On what things are we to set our minds, according to this passage?*

   B. *What is the reason for doing so?*

   C. *What promise is given in verse 4?*

3. Read Hebrews 12:2–3.

   A. *On what are we to fix our eyes, according to this passage? Why?*

   B. *What happens when we don't comply with this command, according to verse 3? Have you ever experienced such consequences? Explain.*

4. Read 1 Corinthians 2:9.

   A. *What kind of God do we serve, according to this verse?*

LET US PRAY

Regardless of the time of year when you read this, get a copy of Handel's *Messiah* and play the "Hallelujah Chorus." Listen carefully to the words and soak in the surging, powerful music. Then spend some time praising God for who he is and thanking him for what he has done for you. Thank him that he will continue to be a powerful, glorious King in your life and that one day his power and glory and kingdom will be apparent for the entire universe to see.

CHAPTER 15

A HOME FOR YOUR HEART

LET US PONDER

1. If you could ask God for one thing, what would you request?

   A. *Answer Max's question above. Why would you ask for this thing?*

   B. *How different would your answer have been ten years ago? Explain.*

2. David craves to remain in the aura, in the atmosphere, in the awareness that he is in God's house wherever he is.

   A. *Do you share David's craving? If so, how do you express this craving? If not, why not?*

   B. *Describe the most unusual place you've ever been in God's house. What happened?*

3. Day by day, I'm learning to live in the Great House of God.

   A. *Do you live more in God's house than you did five years ago? Explain.*

   B. *What is so important about the day-by-day phrase above? What is important about the "I'm learning" portion of the statement? What do both of these things imply about living in the Great House of God? How should this be an encouragement to us all?*

LET US PREPARE

1. In what way is God "a home for your heart"? How does the Lord's Prayer help you to live in that home?

2. Read Psalm 27:1–5.

   A. *What claims does David make in this passage?*

   B. *What does this passage tell you about David's deepest desires?*

   C. *What can you learn from David's example here?*

3. Read John 14:23.

   A. *According to this verse, what is required for us to make our home with God?*

   B. *What promise is given here? Have you taken advantage of this promise? Explain.*

4. Read Acts 17:28.

   A. *What does this verse tell us about having a relationship with God? Do you have this kind of relationship? If so, describe it.*

B. *What does it mean to live in God? What does it mean to move in God? What does it mean to have one's being in God? What does it mean to be one of God's offspring?*

C. *How is this verse a fitting summary of the main point of* The Great House of God?

LET US PRAY

Read through the entire Lord's Prayer one more time (Matt. 6:9–13). As you read, think through the various "rooms" that exist there. Then pray through the prayer, entering each room and relating each one to the events and challenges and triumphs of your life. Begin with praise, end with praise, and in between make your most urgent requests known to God, both for yourself and for others.

The Lucado Reader's Guide

Discover . . . Inside every book by Max Lucado, you'll find words of encouragement and inspiration that will draw you into a deeper experience with Jesus and treasures for your walk with God. What will you discover?

3:16: The Numbers of Hope
. . . the 26 words that can change your life.
core scripture: John 3:16

And the Angels Were Silent
. . . what Jesus Christ's final days can teach you about what matters most.
core scripture: Matthew 20–27

The Applause of Heaven
. . . the secret to a truly satisfying life.
core scripture: The Beatitudes, Matthew 5:1–10

Come Thirsty
. . . how to rehydrate your heart and sink into the wellspring of God's love.
core scripture: John 7:37–38

Cure for the Common Life
. . . the unique things God designed you to do with your life.
core scripture: 1 Corinthians 12:7

Facing Your Giants
. . . when God is for you, no challenge is too great.
core scripture: 1 and 2 Samuel

Fearless
. . . how faith is the antidote to the fear in your life.
core scripture: John 14:1, 3

A Gentle Thunder
. . . the God who will do whatever it takes to lead his children back to him.
core scripture: Psalm 81:7

Great Day, Every Day
. . . how living in a purposeful way will help you trust more, stress less.
core scripture: Psalm 118:24

The Great House of God
. . . a blueprint for peace, joy, and love found in the Lord's Prayer.
core scripture: The Lord's Prayer, Matthew 6:9–13

God Came Near
. . . a love so great that it left heaven to become part of your world.
core scripture: John 1:14

He Chose the Nails
. . . a love so deep that it chose death on a cross—just to win your heart.
core scripture: 1 Peter 1:18–20

He Still Moves Stones
. . . the God who still does the impossible—in your life.
core scripture: Matthew 12:20

In the Eye of the Storm
. . . peace in the storms of your life.
core scripture: John 6

In the Grip of Grace
. . . the greatest gift of all—the grace of God.
core scripture: Romans

It's Not About Me
. . . why focusing on God will make sense of your life.
core scripture: 2 Corinthians 3:18

Just Like Jesus
. . . a life free from guilt, fear, and anxiety.
core scripture: Ephesians 4:23–24

A Love Worth Giving
. . . how living loved frees you to love others.
core scripture: 1 Corinthians 13

Next Door Savior
. . . a God who walked life's hardest trials—and still walks with you through yours.
core scripture: Matthew 16:13–16

No Wonder They Call Him the Savior
. . . hope in the unlikeliest place—upon the cross.
core scripture: Romans 5:15

Outlive Your Life
. . . that a great God created you to do great things.
core scripture: Acts 1

Six Hours One Friday
. . . forgiveness and healing in the middle of loss and failure.
core scripture: John 19–20

Traveling Light
. . . the power to release the burdens you were never meant to carry.
core scripture: Psalm 23

When God Whispers Your Name
. . . the path to hope in knowing that God knows you, never forgets you, and cares about the details of your life.
core scripture: John 10:3

When Christ Comes
. . . why the best is yet to come.
core scripture: 1 Corinthians 15:23

Recommended reading if you're struggling with . . .

FEAR AND WORRY
Come Thirsty
Fearless
For the Tough Times
Next Door Savior
Traveling Light

DISCOURAGEMENT
He Still Moves Stones
Next Door Savior

GRIEF/DEATH OF A LOVED ONE
Next Door Savior
Traveling Light
When Christ Comes
When God Whispers Your Name

GUILT
In the Grip of Grace
Just Like Jesus

LONELINESS
God Came Near

SIN
Facing Your Giants
He Chose the Nails
Six Hours One Friday

WEARINESS
When God Whispers Your Name

Recommended reading if you want to know more about . . .

THE CROSS
And the Angels Were Silent
He Chose the Nails
No Wonder They Call Him the Savior
Six Hours One Friday

GRACE
He Chose the Nails
In the Grip of Grace

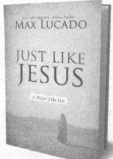

HEAVEN
The Applause of Heaven
When Christ Comes

SHARING THE GOSPEL
God Came Near
No Wonder They Call Him the Savior

Recommended reading if you're looking for more . . .

COMFORT
For the Tough Times
He Chose the Nails
Next Door Savior
Traveling Light

COMPASSION
Outlive Your Life

COURAGE
Facing Your Giants
Fearless

HOPE
3:16: The Numbers of Hope
Facing Your Giants
A Gentle Thunder
God Came Near

JOY
The Applause of Heaven
Cure for the Common Life
When God Whispers Your Name

LOVE
Come Thirsty
A Love Worth Giving
No Wonder They Call Him the Savior

PEACE
And the Angels Were Silent
The Great House of God
In the Eye of the Storm
Traveling Light

SATISFACTION
And the Angels Were Silent
Come Thirsty
Cure for the Common Life
Great Day, Every Day

TRUST
A Gentle Thunder
It's Not About Me
Next Door Savior

Max Lucado books make great gifts!
If you're coming up to a special occasion, consider one of these.

FOR ADULTS:
For the Tough Times
Grace for the Moment
Live Loved
The Lucado Life Lessons Study Bible
Mocha with Max
DaySpring Daybrighteners® and cards

FOR TEENS/GRADUATES:
Let the Journey Begin
You Can Be Everything God Wants You to Be
You Were Made to Make a Difference

FOR KIDS:
Just in Case You Ever Wonder
The Oak Inside the Acorn
You Are Special

FOR PASTORS AND TEACHERS:
God Thinks You're Wonderful
You Changed My Life

AT CHRISTMAS:
The Crippled Lamb
Christmas Stories from Max Lucado
God Came Near

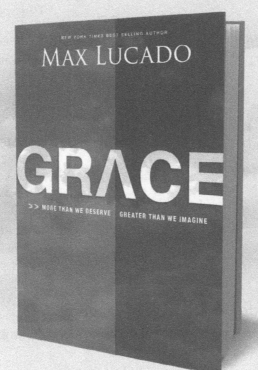

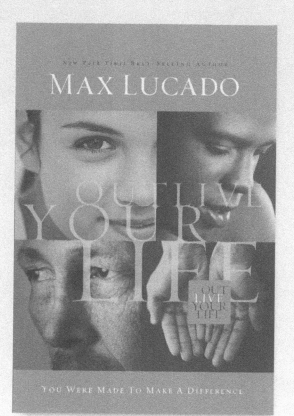

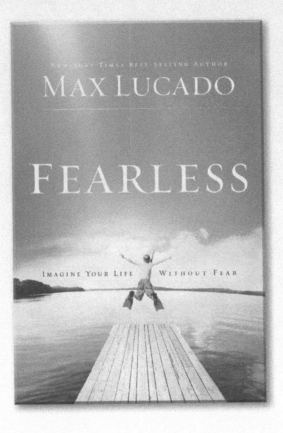

Hope. Pure and simple.

The Teaching Ministry of Max Lucado

UpWords brings to radio and the Internet a message of hope, pure and simple, in Jesus Christ!

Visit www.maxlucado.com to find FREE valuable resources for spiritual growth and encouragement, such as:

- Archives of UpWords, Max's daily radio program. You will also find a listing of radio stations and broadcast times in your area.
- Daily devotionals
- Book excerpts
- Exclusive features and presentations
- Subscription information on how you can receive e-mail messages from Max
- Downloads of audio, video, and printed material
- Ways to receive mobile content

You will also find an online store and special offers.

www.MaxLucado.com

1-800-822-9673

UpWords Ministries
P.O. Box 692170
San Antonio, TX 78269-2170